The Man
In The

The Man In The Fiery FURNACE

By Freddie Sun

WITH MARK AND TAMARA MULVAHILL

"The crucible is for silver and
the furnace for gold but the
Lord tests the heart."
— Proverbs 17:3

Sun Publications
P.O. Box 9037
Charlottesville, Virginia 22906 USA

Paperback:
First printing: October 2000

Contents

Chapter 1

The Empty Man

I was staring up at the clear night sky, marveling at the unusually bright stars, when I suddenly remembered it was Christmas Eve. Until that moment, it had not even occurred to me. But that was not unusual in my circumstance, for times and seasons often lose meaning in prison. I was serving a fifteen-year sentence of hard labor in a Communist Chinese prison camp. The weeks and months jumbled together in a dim, dusty procession in the prison's steel smelting plant, and I, like most prisoners, had lost the will to mark time as free men do.

I had just finished the afternoon shift in the plant. It had been a tiring day; loading and unloading a scorching steel smelting furnace from two in the afternoon until ten at night. I crossed the prison yard and headed towards the bathhouse, my feet crunching the frozen ground beneath. I showered and changed into a clean prison uniform, lingering a moment before leaving the warm bathhouse to go back into the cold night air.

"Hey 390, get over here! And hurry!" A guard yelled at me impatiently while the men crowded each other into a jagged line outside.

As my eyes adjusted to the darkness, I could see the electric barbed wire fence on top of the prison walls surrounding me. An icy chill came over me and I pulled my collar up tightly around my neck. I pressed my way into the line as the searchlights roamed the crowded prison yard and the guards peered down at us from their high towers above.

As I waited to be led back to my prison cell, my mind began traveling to Christmases past. I thought of the tall, lighted tree that had adorned the main hall of the boarding school near Boston where I had spent a year studying as a boy. I remembered visiting Time Square in New York that Christmas and how all the beautiful lights and decorations had made such an impression on me. I thought of the Christmas's in China just after the Communists came into power, before they had begun to persecute the churches. I had sung in a church choir. As I was thinking on these things, the words of the old

Christmas Carols came to my mind, and looking up at the stars twinkling in the sky I shut out everything around me and began to quietly sing. I sang one song after another. They poured out from deep in my heart.

In spite of the darkness surrounding me, I could not remember a time when I had had more peace. Under the circumstances it seemed quite out of place. I thought about my situation and what a sight I must have made. My hair was completely shaved off, I wore the sloppy linen uniform of a prisoner, and I was forced to do slave labor eight hours a day. My parents had practically disowned me. I was no longer considered a respected member of their family. I was separated by over 300 miles from my wife and children. My family life had been reduced to twenty-minute visits from my wife twice a year. My home was gone. It had long ago been ransacked and confiscated. I no longer had a career as a geologist. I had been expelled from the Chinese Academy of Sciences, having received an official discharge from my work assignment, which would black list me for life. After prison I could only look forward to a menial job. Instead of a name, I had a number. I suffered from asthma and pleurisy. Nothing remained for me in this life. I had lost all things. In the eyes of the world I was an empty man.

But God's Spirit was strong upon me, and inwardly I was enjoying an abundant life. I had lost all that is valued by this world, but had found riches in Jesus Christ. I began to realize how little real value the material things are to a man. Everyday I walked with Jesus and He never abandoned me. He had brought me here to be emptied of myself.

I thought of how Job must have felt. God had allowed him to lose all things to test his faithfulness. As Job sat covered with dust and ashes he declared, " The Lord gave and the Lord has taken away. May the name of the Lord be praised." Now I also had the opportunity to repent in dust and ashes. God had placed the dust of scrap iron and the ashes of melted steel in my life. He was allowing me to pass through the refiner's fire so that I would be made ready for use by the Master. He had only "taken away" in order for me to receive a greater blessing. And on this lonely Christmas Eve so far from family and friends, He had given me the greatest blessing of all, the gift of Himself. I knew that He had a purpose for my life. And all that had happened to me to this point was part of His great and unfolding plan. I thought back, about the family I had been born into, and the events that had shaped my life, beginning with the adventure to America when I was twelve years old.

Chapter 2

Beginning

"Look at all the cars up there!" I cried. My mother, who obviously lacked a twelve-year-old boy's enthusiasm for such things, only smiled and patted my head in acknowledgement. We stood watching a new world unfold before us from the deck of the large ocean liner that had carried us from our ancient homeland of China to the shores of modern America. I had heard many times of the wonders of this great country, with its tall skyscrapers, and paved highways teeming with automobiles. My parents had still been very fond of America at this time and had told me many fascinating stories about it. We sailed under the famous Golden Gate Bridge and I ran to the ship's railing straining for a better view.

My mother continued standing quietly, with a far-away look in her eyes. No doubt she was remembering years ago when she had made this same journey as a young college student. There were many Chinese students on that voyage. The men had far outnumbered the women. At that time very few Chinese women even attended college. Both my father and mother were on the boat, though they didn't know each other yet. In fact my mother hadn't even noticed him among all the eligible young men. Later on however, at a summer camp for students, they met each other and quickly fell in love. After they completed their education, they returned to China. And in 1928, two years after their return, they were married.

My father was a banker, having studied Finance at New York's Columbia University while in the United States. For a country boy from a poor family, he was considered very successful. He had lost his mother at a young age and only acquired an education through hard work and the help of scholarships. He had graduated from China's Ching Hua University, a very distinguished school, before going on to Graduate School in New York. The Chinese government founded Ching Hua University after the Boxer Rebellion. They had been forced to pay remuneration to the eight countries that had quelled the rebellion, and the United States used its portion to provide scholarships for Ching Hua University graduates to further their studies in America.

We lived very well by Chinese standards. My parents were always busy with their careers, so the responsibility of raising me fell mostly on our servants. I remember my father as a kind man, but always solemn and distant.

"Freddie," he would often say, "you need to study hard in school if you want to be successful like me. When I was your age we didn't have servants. I had to do all the chores, and then my studies."

The western influence on my mother went back several generations to her grandfather. Through unusual circumstances he had received a western education in England. The story had been told many times in our family, how my great grandfather had lost his parents during the Tai Ping rebellion of 1851 and had been adopted by a British general.

"General Gordon Sir, I found this lad amongst the refugees, he seemed a winsome sort, and I know how you care for these lads," said the soldier, as he stood erect with his hand still on the boy. The General looked up over his glasses and put down his pen. With the look of one accustomed to command, he studied the boy for a moment. "What is your name, son?"

Imitating the soldier my great grandfather replied smartly, "Wang, General Gordon, Sir!"

This amused the General and soon the boy became one of his favorites. General Gordon had a very benevolent heart and helped many of the destitute orphan boys that he found in China. He even adopted some of them and took them to England to be educated. My great grandfather, William Wang Quincey, as General Gordon later renamed him was among them and benefited greatly from this advantage.

He returned to China after completing his education and settled in Hong Kong where he obtained a position at the police headquarters. In those days, only British personnel were assigned to headquarters so this was a great privilege. He was the first Chinese citizen allowed to work there. He advanced quickly in his career and eventually went on to found the modern police system in China. He was very brave and once while chasing an armed robber he jumped from the second floor to tackle the man. My brother, cousins, and I were very impressed by this story as boys and we used to make believe we were my great grandfather catching the criminal. We would take turns jumping off the stairs, one higher than the next, until we were up to the second floor. It's a wonder that we didn't break a leg or worse!

Great Grandfather Quincey greatly admired the British but lived like a Chinese gentleman of the feudalistic tradition. He had four wives who raised six sons and five daughters. Several of the daughters married westerners.

My mother, who had been influenced by my great grandfather, had always planned to study abroad when her time came. She was born in Hong Kong, but most of her childhood was spent in Singapore where her father was also a banker. Later she returned to China and attended a missionary school. Upon completion she entered Ching Hua University and began preparing to go to the United States to complete her studies. She majored in history at both Wellesley College and Columbia University. She was a very liberated woman for that time in China, and worked in her profession for her entire life.

The way I made my arrival into the world should have been a sign to my mother that I was going to cause her periods of discomfort in life. She was an extremely petite woman, and suffered nine days of labor before I finally arrived on February 13, 1936. The exhilarating experience of being born must have taken it out of me. I was unable to breathe at first for a dangerously long time. The doctor did the usual thing of turning me upside down and hitting my bottom. But when that didn't work, she put me alternately in hot and then cold water until at last I began to breathe. I was being amply repaid for the nine days of misery I had caused my mother. It was also a sign of things to come. I was "persecuted" from the moment I came into this world!

"He's so fat! How favored you are Agnes to have another son. But what shall I name him?" My grandfather held me up. As part of the influence of his background, he had the custom of giving all the grandchildren western names. " Well, Agnes my last two grandsons were named after British kings, but I think we need a good German king to go with a fat one like this. I know, King Frederick of Germany, He's fat enough to be this one's namesake." So I received the name Frederick, which was quickly shortened to just plain Freddie.

In those days it was commonly thought that a fat baby meant a healthy baby. However, that was certainly not true in my case. My childhood seemed to be plagued by one illness after another. When I was two years old I became seriously ill with a very high fever. I couldn't sleep for three days and nights and had convulsions. I was very close to dying and needed a miracle. At the time my mother attended church but did not have a personal relationship with Jesus. But God in his mercy had brought a Believer into our family. My mother's younger brother had married a woman named Grace Wang. She was a committed Christian and suggested that she and my mother pray for my recovery. They did, and I soon improved. Throughout my childhood the seed of the gospel was planted in me and continually nurtured by my Auntie Grace. I owe her a debt that I can never repay.

"Freddie, Freddie, wake up," my nanny gently called to me. "It's time for your medicine."

I awoke to the very familiar scene of my nanny, Lin, standing over me like a nurse examining her patient. Obediently I opened my mouth and swallowed down the vile tasting concoction with a shudder. I was recovering from another asthma attack, a chronic illness I suffered all during my childhood. I had developed asthma at the age of four after contracting Pneumonia and almost dying. Growing up I spent many weary days in bed, propped up with pillows to make my breathing easier. During my attacks I couldn't eat or lie down. My breathing was so heavy that it sounded like bellows, and I often coughed so hard that I would see stars before my eyes. But God had His hand on me. And eventually even the asthma would work for the good in my life. Even as a child I was learning to persevere in the face of hardship. It was helping me to develop character. I had to push myself to keep going no matter how bad I felt, in order to keep up with others.

Since I spent so much time in bed I developed a love for reading. My parents had an extensive library, and I would read all kinds of books, even ones well above my age level. Detective stories were my favorite though. They triggered my imagination, and I would spend hours day dreaming. I could picture myself catching villainous criminals, just like my great grandfather had done. Sometimes I was a great soccer star, leading my team to victory, and scoring the winning goal. Other times I dreamed of being a famous politician rising to become the leader of China. I was always an optimist about the future.

Although my asthma had often kept me bound to the narrow perimeters of my bedroom, it was to eventually become my ticket to travel across the world. When I was eleven years old my mother was asked to return to Wellesley College in Boston to teach Chinese history. It was a very high honor for her to have been chosen. My mother was very career minded, and my father was in full agreement that she should take advantage of this special opportunity. One of my aunts suggested to her that she take me along to see if the change in climate could improve my asthma. I of course was thrilled, and soon we were on our way to America.

The long ocean voyage had finally come to an end as we now headed into the great San Francisco harbor. I would experience life in America for the next full year. It would change my perspective forever and prove invaluable to me years later when I faced the deceptive power of Communist propaganda.

Chapter 3

Fessenden

"All Aboard!" the conductor's voice bellowed over the din of the crowded station.

My mother and I gave quick parting hugs to our relatives, clustering around us. They had come to see us off at the train. We were leaving Chicago after a short visit, beginning the last leg of our journey from San Francisco to Boston.

As the train pulled slowly away from the station, my mind was full of all the many things we had seen along the way. Our train had climbed from the white salt covered earth surrounding the Great Salt Lake to the snow covered peaks of the Rocky Mountains. I was impressed by so much natural beauty. But what caught my attention most were the many modern homes and buildings, and the wide neatly paved streets all teeming with automobiles. It seemed to me that everyone owned a car. This was strange for me because in China only very few could afford automobiles. Our family did not own one, but because my father was the bank president, he had use of the bank's chauffeured driven car. Chicago's noisy subways had also fascinated me. It was a thrill to watch the trains speed along and then suddenly disappear underground only to quickly reappear on the street, a block away.

I was enjoying the time alone with my mother and all the special attention I was receiving. She too seemed very happy, and I'm sure she was thinking a great deal about the challenging days ahead as a visiting professor at Wellesley. Normally I spent very little time with her. She was both a college professor and the head of the YWCA in China and this left very little time for her family. Since most of my care and upbringing had been left to our servants, I had become very independent at an early age. But like any young boy I still craved affection and made the most of this special time together. I knew that it would come to an end soon enough.

"You'll like boarding school Freddie, you'll see." My mother repeatedly assured me as we neared Boston. I wasn't so sure, but I set aside those thoughts for later. I was having too much fun to think about that now.

In Boston, my mother and I quickly settled into life at Wellesley. She was given a two-room apartment on the second floor of the girl's dorm. I stayed with her until it was time to attend the boarding school, and discovered the privileges of being the only boy living in a girl's dorm. In those days the men were forbidden to go upstairs to pick up their dates. They had to wait in the lobby while the girl was summoned. But of course this did not apply to a twelve year old boy, and I took great delight in striding past my male counterparts, their eyes following me as I marched triumphantly up the stairs.

The girls in the dorm doted on me, treating me like a spoiled pet. They often took me with them to the movies and to eat ice cream. My mother was always happy for me to go, since she needed time to grade papers and make lesson plans for her Oriental History classes.

Miss Williams, the professor at Wellesley who had invited my mother to teach, arranged for my schooling. Through her influence I was able to attend an exclusive Christian boy's school nearby, called Fessenden .The tuition at that time was $2000 a year, but Miss Williams helped me to get a partial scholarship, reducing the cost to only $500. I can see now that God opened this door for me. At the time I was still very unaware of the hand of God on my life. But years later the seed of Christ's love that was planted in me at this time would take root.

The first day of school soon arrived, and Miss Williams drove my mother and I there. I was very nervous, because not only was I the new kid in school, I was also the new kid in the country. I had already discovered that my English left much to be desired. I had studied English in my grade school in Shanghai, but the few words I had learned out of a book, were now very little help. It seemed to me I would never be able to understand these people who talked so fast.

My mother helped me to find my room. And as she prepared to leave, I felt a sudden heaviness in my heart.

"Now Freddie, you be a good boy and mind your teachers. I'll be back to see you in just a couple of months on the first parent visiting day." My mother spoke with her usual reserve, for emotions were things that we often kept hidden. But I thought my mother's eyes looked just a little moist behind her glasses, and I admit I had to swallow hard to get the lump in my throat to go away.

After she had left, I must have looked very lonely, sitting with my feet dangling over the edge of the big solid framed bed; my little suitcase plopped down beside me. I looked around at the sparse little cubicle that was my new bedroom. Other than the bed, the only other furnishings were a desk and dresser, which fit snugly against the opposite wall. The excited voices of the other boys could be heard over the partitions, but I was too shy to try to make friends just then. That night I cried myself to sleep.

The next morning I awoke feeling tired from a restless sleep and anxious about my first day of school. I hurried to class dressed in my best pair of slacks and new shirt, hoping to make a good, first impression. Ten minutes later, feeling quite foolish, I was back in my room changing into my blue suit. I had been unprepared for the formality of Fessenden. That afternoon I didn't dare take off my suit, though I had noticed that all my classmates were now dressed more casually. But I was determined to play it safe, until later when one of my teachers finally pulled me aside and gently asked me why I was still wearing my suit.

The first few weeks of classes were very difficult. I had to work extra hard to make up for my poor English. But the librarian tutored me every afternoon, and in just three months, I understood English quite well and was able to keep up with my fellow classmates. We had a rigorous schedule: classes in the morning, sports in the afternoon, and study hall in the evening. But I adjusted quickly and soon loved it there.

Many prominent families put their children into Fessenden to receive a high quality Christian education. Franklin Roosevelt's grandson was one of my classmates. Even though most of the children were from wealthy homes, strict rules required that all the children receive the same stringent allowance. We were each given exactly fifty cents a week. But back then a kid could make fifty cents stretch pretty far if he had to. Cokes only cost a dime, and there was a wide range of toys and trinkets at the local "Five and Dime" that were great for boys. However, I still found that my "needs" often exceeded my income, and so I was delighted when an opportunity arose to earn more money.

"Do we have any volunteers to serve the food?"

My head had popped up as soon as I heard the headmistress begin to question to the class. Immediately my hand shot up. Mrs. Gibson looked around the room. "Ok, we'll let Tommy, John, Frank, Mark, and Timothy be our servers today."

My heart sank. I realized of course, I had already been chosen to help serve the food the last four days running. But I had a deep longing to serve, not to mention that helping at dinnertime or washing the dishes afterwards earned us points towards a half-day holiday in town with fifty cents to spend however we wanted. And that meant I could go to the Saturday afternoon matinee and still have enough left over for popcorn or ice cream. Even though we were shown two movies every Saturday night at the school, it didn't seem like enough, and I always wanted more.

Fessenden was a Christian School, and God used it to plant seeds of the Gospel in my life that year. My teachers were very kind, but strict, and their concern for me touched me deeply. We had to attend church in our blue suits every Sunday, but I never got very much out of it. The American boys didn't seem to pay much attention either. Possibly for me it was the language barrier, or it may have been that the preacher wasn't able to reach the hearts of little boys. But the love that I experienced made a strong impression on me.

My mother also had many Christian friends whom reached out to us and showed us God's love. And although I didn't have much interest in the Bible at that time, since it was so hard for me to understand, the Christian kindness spoke volumes to my heart. God's love is a language that all foreigners understand.

But life was about to take another new turn, and I would soon discover how my experiences in America that year were to have such an important affect on my life.

Chapter 4

The Communists

I sat on my suitcase again, this time determined to get it to shut. I had already taken out two model cars and a stack of old comic books, and I wasn't about to sacrifice anything else. It was upsetting enough to have to be packing to leave.

My adventure in America had been suddenly cut short by some unexpected events. The disgruntling news had come to me only a short time earlier in a letter from my mother. I had completed my first year at Fessenden and was spending the summer in Cape Cod at a private boy's camp, organized by the school.

I remember the day I received the letter, it had begun so well. I had spent the morning learning to sail, followed by archery practice. For lunch we had been served delicious grilled hamburgers, topped off with a large dish of my favorite ice cream. The afternoon would be filled with baseball and swimming. This was the life for a boy. As far as I was concerned, there was no reason to ever go back to China.

I was relaxing on my bunk after lunch, enjoying the soft coastal breeze coming through our cabin window when I suddenly remembered my mother's letter, which had come that morning. I opened it hoping for some news about my father and brother, knowing that they would soon be visiting us. However, as I read the letter my heart began to sink.

"Dear Freddie," my mother wrote, "I have some urgent news. Your father called and told me that he and your brother will not be able to visit us as planned. There has been some unrest in China and a new political opposition group has taken over the government. They are called Communists. Your father says that they are promising to bring about many needed reforms and from what he has said I think that they maybe the answer to China's problems. And they favor women's rights, which I think is wonderful. Also you know that it has been so recent that both of your grandfathers have passed away and your father thought it would be good for the family to be together again. So

I'm afraid you will not be attending Fessenden next year. I have resigned from my teaching position at Wellesley, and we will be returning to China at the end of August."

I put down the letter, and while battling my emotions, tried desperately to think of a way that I could somehow stay. But I knew that my parents would never allow it, and to be honest, I wasn't sure that I was ready for that much separation from my family. I had to accept it, we would soon be returning to China. But it was frustrating, for what did I care about some new political party that would probably be kicked out again in a year or two?

When we had left China the Communists were still far from Shanghai and had seemed quite insignificant. We had not even considered them a threat. They had risen very slowly in power. At the beginning of the 20th century, China had still been very much rooted in the past. The government during this time was corrupt and very weak. The Chinese people were still bound to many centuries old customs, which were stifling their progress as a nation. The younger generation began to look for ways to modernize China. After the fall of the dynasty in 1911, there were power struggles among different groups, each promising to bring about a government, which would be able to solve China's problems. At the forefront, a group later known as the Nationalists was espousing Democracy. In 1927 they came into power. However, about this same time, a party was formed which adopted the ideals of Communism. They hoped to achieve what they viewed as "the success" of the revolution in Russia. The Nationalist government was soon engaged in a power struggle with the Communists for control of the country. The Nationalists eventually won out and drove the Communists far into Northern China.

In the 1930's the Japanese invaded and conquered much of the territory of China. The Nationalist government continued to hang on during these years, but because the Japanese as well as various Chinese Warlords were competing with them for territory and power, they failed to bring about any real Democratic reforms.

After World War II, the allied forces defeated the Japanese. But in Northeast China the Soviet Red Army had remained behind to help the Chinese Communists who were now making great military advances against the Nationalists. The Communists gained power through lawless means, even promising to give the peasants the property belonging to the landlords. They made tremendous strides in just a few years and by 1949 they had literally driven the Nationalists completely out of China. The Nationalist government retreated to the island of Taiwan.

Our trip home to China was long and difficult. The political situation had greatly complicated things. The ousted Nationalist government blockaded the mouth of the Yangtze River where our ship needed to enter to reach Shanghai. So we were forced to come ashore in Hong Kong and wait three months for another ship. When one finally came available, it carried us right past our destination of Shanghai all the way to Tianjin in northern China. From there we traveled back by train to Shanghai, and to a long awaited reunion with my father and brother.

The lure of Communism on my parents was strange considering the benefits western capitalism had already afforded them. Not only was our family heritage strongly tied to the West but both my parents had successful careers due in large part to their receiving an education in America. However, the Communists were very deceiving. They would say whatever they thought people wanted to hear in order to win favor over the Nationalists. Most likely it was out of fear that my parents so readily embraced Communism. Anyone remaining loyal to the Nationalists was now an enemy of the state. So like most others, my parents willingly accepted the new government without question and determined to make the best of it.

All privately owned banks including my fathers' were consolidated and placed under the central control of the Communists. Because of his experience and qualifications they later appointed my father vice president of the newly formed Peoples Bank of Shanghai.

My mother was promoted to dean of a women's university, and was able to continue on as chairwoman of the YWCA. Eventually the YWCA became totally controlled by the Communists, and had little in common with the Christian organization it had once been.

A few months after we returned, the Korean War broke out. China sided with North Korea, and the United States was suddenly portrayed as imperialist. The Soviet Union was viewed as China's big brother, and would lead all of mankind into producing paradise on earth. Those were the honeymoon days between the Soviets and the Chinese. Every movie house issued forth a continual stream of Soviet propaganda films. The Communists claimed that most of the people in the United States lived in poverty and that the Capitalists were always exploiting them.

For me it was impossible to believe that the country where I had just lived, and come to admire so much, was now my enemy. Of course, I knew that the Communists were lying, since I had seen the prosperity in America with my own eyes. So I became quite vocal in my views. But I was just a boy and had no career to protect, nor family to concern myself with, and no real understanding of how ruthless the Communists could be. However I soon found myself at odds with my family.

Now that I was back in China, my asthma returned, and once again I found myself spending lots of time in bed, recovering from respiratory attacks. I had a short wave radio that I had brought back with me from the United States, and I would listen to American baseball and football games on the Voice of America. Gradually I grew interested in the news programs as well. And as I heard the reporting about the Korean War, I compared it to what the Communists were saying and I became increasingly uneasy about this new government. I wondered what the future would hold.

There were many changes occurring throughout the country. Among these, Christianity, which still had very little influence in China, was now at odds with the ideology of Communism. My parents, who had never been overly committed to attending church regularly, now abandoned the custom altogether. It is interesting however to look back on how God faithfully worked to keep church a part of my life. I had a good friend who lived next door named Paul Lin. We had developed a secret knock that we used to communicate with each other through the walls of our connecting houses. I could signal to him and he would come over to visit me when I was too sick to get up. We would play chess, and all kinds of other games, spending long hours together. I would be propped up on my pillows at one end of the bed, and Paul would be hunched over and sitting cross-legged on the other end. Paul was a very gentle and kind person. He was a Christian, and would often invite me to go to church with him.

"Do you think your parents will let you go to church with me Sunday?" Paul's way of asking always made church seem a little more exciting than I had remembered it. But he knew by now that I would come, despite my parent's disapproval, and maybe even a little because of it. Unfortunately God was still far from my thoughts at this time, though He was graciously at work in my life during those years.

As time went on it became obvious to my parents that I did not view things quite like them or my older brother. The more they became immersed in Communism, the more we conflicted. Finally, they decided that firmer measures must be taken so that I would learn to appreciate the benefits of this new enlightened philosophy. They decided that Shanghai was still too "western" in culture for me to become well grounded in Communism. I was sent to live with my Uncle Gordon and Aunt Grace who had relocated to Beijing. They believed that in Beijing, since it was the capitol and right under the nose of Chairman Mao, I would eventually see the light and would be converted. I did, in fact, end up being converted, but it was a different sort of conversion than my parents had in mind. It had apparently escaped them (and I believe God had His hand in this) that Aunt Grace who had earlier lived near us in Shanghai, was a devout Christian, and had been witnessing to me the whole time I was growing up. In their vain attempt to get me to accept Communism, my parents had placed me in the home of the person most responsible for getting me to accept Christ.

Chapter 5

Born Again

"We must remain separate from government control," cried Pastor Wang Mintao, "Christ is the Head of the Church, not man!"

He paused, and began looking slowly around at the faces in the large crowded church. A strange hush came over the great hall as though the whole church at that moment suddenly realized for the first time the full gravity of their situation. I sat in the back, and stared in awe at this bold man, amazed at his words. I had never heard anyone speak this way before about the Communists. Certainly he knew they had spies in the crowd!

The church I was in just happened to be located right across the street from where I was now living with my aunt Grace. So not only was

I being witnessed to daily by my Christian Aunt, but I was now sitting under one of the most well known, outspoken, and influential preachers in China. Almost 1000 people attended his church every Sunday. The narrow street between the church and my aunt's home was only about 30 feet wide, and every Sunday morning the fervent singing from the church came right into my bedroom. There was no escaping it. But the sound of the congregation singing so joyfully began to have its' affect on me, and it was not long before I was attending the church.

Pastor Wang's teaching had also attracted me. It awakened something in my soul. And like him, I wasn't very pleased with this new government either. I hadn't wanted to leave Shanghai. I missed my old friends and my parents' comfortable, three -story home. Beijing at this time wasn't the modern city it is now and I despised living in this dirty backward place. I felt superior to almost everyone here since I was from Shanghai, and a return student from overseas at that.

Of course, Pastor Wang's reasons for not liking the Communists were much nobler, and for that I felt a little ashamed. Also he was risking his own safety, by warning the church of the diabolical scheme brewing by the Communists.

They were using very subtle means, and by mixing truth with lies, were attempting to replace Jesus Christ with Chairman Mao, as the Head of the church.

At this time the Korean War was still going on and anti-western sentiment was at it's strongest. Western missionaries were fleeing the country and the church was at a crossroads. The Communists demanded that churches cut off all relations with the West, including financial assistance. Exploiting the truth that the church should not develop dependency on the West, they initiated what was called the Three-Self Patriotic Movement (TSPM). The three main tenants of this new movement stated that the church should be self-supporting, self-governing, and self-propagating. The concept itself was not bad. The goal of every missionary should be to relinquish control as soon as possible to the leadership of the newly planted church. The problem was that the Communists had no intention of allowing the church to control itself, they wanted to control it. However they were not strong enough yet to fully exert their authority and had to compromise by giving the church leaders five years in which to become part of the TSPM.

As part of their dark schemes, the pastor would be authorized and paid by the state, and only allowed to preach what they approved. Believers would only be allowed to meet when and where the government permitted. And evangelism and new church planting was generally prohibited. Of course these things were never stated so bluntly. They acted slyly in those days as if they wanted to be friends with the church, but their true motive was to weaken the church and then destroy it.

Throughout my high school years, Pastor Wang's sermons and writings were having an effect on me, and for the first time I began to think seriously about God. Also my aunt Grace in her own gentle way frequently talked to me about giving my life to Christ.

"You know Freddie that I will always love you no matter what you choose," she would always begin this way and I knew what was coming, "but I will never be at peace until I see our whole family come to Jesus."

I would listen respectfully, as was expected by my elders. But I was not ready to give up my life to become some religious outcast. In high school I had become arrogant and proud and had developed a rather worldly life-style. I now smoked and drank, and had a habit of stealing money from my parents so I could do all the things that I wanted to do with my friends. I knew all that would have to change if I were to follow Christ. Not only that, now was not a very safe time in China to be a Christian. Pastor Wang and others were warning that a time was coming when people would be persecuted just for being Christians.

My only desire at this time was to graduate and return to Shanghai for medical school. My grades were very good, but I had one problem. I had attended high school in Beijing. The new government wanted to fill up the universities of the North, so they made a ruling that anyone who had attended high school in the North would have to attend a university in the North. But I was stubborn and arrogant, and ignored the ruling. I decided to try for a university in Shanghai anyway, even though it was in the South. So on the college entrance exam I requested only medical schools in Shanghai. In those days college assignments were published in a national newspaper, and I remember the shock I received the afternoon the results were published. I had picked up the paper on my way home from school, but decided not to look at it until I was alone. I got home and raced up to my room.

"Is that you Freddie?" I heard my Aunt calling from the kitchen. I ignored her knowing she would want to ask me about my assignment before I had a chance to look at it. It seemed to me that the whole world was waiting to know. I tossed my books on the bed and tore open the newspaper, hurriedly flipping through it until I found the page where the school assignments were listed. My eyes scanned the columns up and down. I did this several times over, thinking I must have somehow missed my name. Then I sat down slowly, still staring at the page in shock. I couldn't believe it; I hadn't even been assigned to any university. What a fool I had made of myself! In the Chinese way of thinking, I had completely lost face.

The next year and a half of my life I underwent a complete transformation. I was now so humbled that when I returned to my parent's home in Shanghai, I withdrew to myself. My parents must have felt sorry for me, because they didn't say a whole lot. My mother set up tutors for me and I studied Chinese literature, as well as various languages, including English (which was my favorite) and Russian. I also put to use my ability as a swimmer, which I had developed at the camp near Fessenden, and found work as a swimming coach.

Those were trying days for me. All my peers had gone off to their respective universities and I had no desire to keep in contact with them. It would have only aggravated my situation to hear about their many wonderful experiences. But something new was happening to me. I found myself turning more and more to the Lord for comfort.

I was attending the same Cantonese Church I had gone to with Paul Lin, and where I had sung in the choir. However, now something had changed in me. I was struggling with what I had learned about the Three Self-Patriotic Movement (TSPM). Pastor Wang had preached so strongly against it, that I wasn't comfortable anymore with the Cantonese church since they had joined this growing movement. I was confused and began to want to know the truth. As I sought God about this matter, I spent more and more time reading the Bible. Pastor Wang had warned us that our Bibles could be taken away from us, and as a result it had become more precious to me. God began to show me from His word the true nature of the TSPM. But as He did, strangely enough I became more aware of my own sin, and need for forgiveness.

One evening I was alone in my bedroom. I had spent the entire day praying and seeking God. It was May 20th 1955. I was sensing God's presence stronger than ever. And suddenly I knew what I had to do. I got down on my knees and with tears welling up in my eyes I confessed to the Lord every sin I could ever think of. I asked Jesus to come into my heart and was filled with a tremendous peace and joy as I realized that I was now truly forgiven. I got up and crumpled in my hand the last pack of cigarettes I would ever buy and threw them in the trashcan.

I knew that the step I had just taken could turn out to be a dangerous one. My aunt Grace had visited Shanghai and told me that Pastor Wang had been arrested, and that my two cousins, Eddie and George had been interrogated. Watchman Nee's church had continued to stay open even though he had been arrested several years earlier. But now the three elders who had remained in charge had been arrested, and the church closed (the Communists later killed one of them, making him a martyr for his faith). The persecutions were forcing everyone to make a decision one way or another. Unfortunately, during this time some denied their faith. But by God's grace there were many others like myself, who for the first time, were now committing themselves to follow Jesus.

Although I was unaware of it at the time, a whole new underground church movement had begun to develop. But for the first eight months as a new Christian I had no one to fellowship with except for Jesus. There wasn't anyone in my church or anyone in Shanghai for that matter that I knew I could confide in about my newfound faith. I had to depend on my own private devotions to stay built up spiritually.

But I was soon to learn that there were many others like myself who no longer wanted to attend churches that had joined the TSPM. God was leading true believers to leave the state-run churches, and to start meeting in homes. And God's hand in this soon became very clear. Within just a few years, all the state-employed pastors were forced to go to work at factories or on labor farms in order to be "retrained" in the correct way of thinking, and their churches were closed. The true motives of the Communists became fully evident, having first weakened the church; they would now destroy it. And it might have worked too, but for the fact that God had saved a remnant who were now hidden all over China in what became known as "the house churches".

Chapter 6

God's Calling

"Shhh!" my aunt whispered, putting her finger to her lips.

We quickly lowered our voices, but kept singing. Smiling nervously at one another, we realized that we had gotten a little too spirited. It was easy to do. The presence of the Lord was so strong and the fellowship with other believers so precious, it was hard not to want to shout!

A small storeroom at the back of my aunt's home had become the meeting place for our new little church. We were one of the many new house-churches that were now springing up all over China. My aunt, my step-grandmother, and I, along with several others made up this small gathering of believers. My uncle was still not a believer, but had allowed my aunt to hold the meetings at their home. The other believers were all former members of Pastor Wang's church. Many of the believers had divided up into small home fellowships after the Communists had closed down the church. The meetings were purposely kept small. It was important that everyone knew and trusted each other. No one could be sure who might turn into an informer. These were dangerous times. Any Christian caught meeting like this faced possible imprisonment and torture.

Once persecution breaks out, the church suddenly finds that most of its meetings become prayer meetings. This one was no different. We began praying, one after another, each person in turn, softly speaking out. We always prayed for many different things, but there were two main prayers that were being repeated all over China. The first was that the Lord would help us to remain faithful. It was no longer easy to be a Christian, and it would be difficult to remain faithful now that our lives were in danger. In fact, we knew we could not do it in our own strength. We needed the strength of the Lord. Our other prayer was that China would one day open up again to the Gospel. We had no idea, at that time; the marvelous way that God would answer that prayer.

I was living with my aunt once again. I had finally been accepted into a university after being tutored at home for what had seemed like the longest year and a half of my life. I was studying physics at a university in Beijing. But now I had a new problem. I didn't like the idea of teaching physics after I was finished with school. The door had been closed for me to study medicine so I had taken what was available without giving it much thought. But I knew that once I graduated and was assigned a position by the government I would have little chance of ever changing my career again. I was still tossing different ideas around of what to do when I met Paul Li. He was a Catholic who was also a born again believer. We hit it off from the start and spent many enjoyable hours together fellowshipping and discussing the Bible. We also discovered that we were both unhappy studying physics. Paul had found out about a university in Nanjing where they taught geology.

"Come on Freddie," I remember him trying to convince me one day, "you would love it, I know. And it offers more courses and a much better opportunity for advancement."

"Paul, I don't know a thing about geology, and I'm sure not interested in studying a bunch of rocks!" I grumped at him, still sore over the fact that I wasn't able to study medicine.

But Paul ignored me, and continued with his usual perseverance. "We would get to travel all over the country to do research. We'll be camping out, hiking, and exploring, it will be like being a Boy Scout for a profession!"

Eventually Paul's arguments and my continuing aversion to teach physics led me to take the entrance exam for Nanjing University. I passed and was accepted. My second venture to Beijing had only lasted three months. But I had two very memorable experiences there. One of course was my Aunt's house church. The second was that I had made close acquaintance with fellow student believers while studying physics. We would secretly meet outside in a park (named interestingly enough "The Temple of Heaven") to study the Bible and encourage one another in the faith. I remember once after it had just snowed, it was so peaceful fellowshipping under the pine trees, with the sun glistening on the snow-covered ground. We had truly sensed the presence of the Lord.

Before long Paul and I were both attending Nanjing University. To my surprise I found that I really enjoyed studying geology. I specialized in Paleontology. I also learned a lot about the theory of evolution during my studies, and am now able to argue all the more persuasively against it.

I lived in a dorm room with 7 other students. They all learned quickly that I was a

Christian because I read my Bible every day and knelt down to pray in the room. I met secretly with four or five other Christians every week for Bible study and prayer. We often met outside and appeared to be studying to all inquiring minds. The Communists were strongly against Christians meeting like this and it was dangerous to share your faith with others. I learned this first hand after encouraging a close friend of mine to bring his problems to the Lord.

My friend Chang had been struggling with many family problems. I told him how the Lord could help him through the difficulties and he had been very interested. However, during this time the Communists in one of their many "movements" to control society were requiring everyone to submit written confessions of any negative thoughts we had about them. They promised us (falsely, as I soon discovered) that it would remain confidential and would never follow us afterwards. Chang was a trusting fellow and without meaning to get me in trouble, confessed to the Communists that I had shared my faith with him. The Communists reacted by gathering all the students together to publicly criticize me. This was now becoming a common practice in society. I was made to stand in front of everyone while they hurled accusations and insults at me. In their eyes, I was anticommunist and rebellious to the government. I only suffered a little humiliation, but it was my first mild taste of what it is like to be persecuted. The commotion had drawn attention to Paul Li and he was also criticized. Afterwards they ordered us not to speak to anyone else about our faith and let us go.

I had found though that the hatred and resentment I had held against the Communists was no longer with me since coming to know the Lord. God had given me a real love and compassion for my adversaries. So in my written confessions I honestly told them about my previous attitude and happily assured them that I no longer felt that way. It was not well received. But in my mind I was quite willing to obey this new government as long as it didn't conflict with God's commandments (which it had the unfortunate habit of doing quite regularly). Even my parents had noticed a change in my attitude and had mistakenly thought that at last I was starting to come around.

However, the damaging results of Communism began to be more clearly seen. At this time the government embarked on what was commonly called the "Steel and Iron Movement". Mao thought that if China could raise its steel and iron production to a hundred million tons per year, that it would become a great industrial power. Since geologists were needed to locate new iron ore sites, they were suddenly considered heroes. Though we were only students at the time, we were expected to find iron ore just the same. We were given free rides to anywhere we needed to go for geological expeditions and were provided with the best food. We had to report on every site that we explored no matter what we discovered. If we even discovered a small trace, hundreds of peasants would be sent out immediately to dig for it. Naturally many times all the digging produced nothing.

A classmate of mine once found iron ore deposits on a hill that bordered two counties. The officials of both counties wanted to be able to claim it as their own, so they each quickly ordered as many peasants as they could find to dig for the iron ore. When the crowd reached 8,000 my friend ran away. There was no way anyone could organize a crowd of that size to do excavation.

Everyone in China was required to help with the steel and iron production. Children gathered scrap metal in the streets, and the peasant farmers left their crops in the fields to work in the great steel mills. Then, in order to begin implementing the "reconstruction of society" to what the Communists had envisioned, all the peasants were moved onto communal farms. The idea was made more palatable because the Communists ruled that all food was to be given away for free. It was not long however, before all the reserves were eaten up. Everyone was working to produce steel, and no one was available to harvest the crops. Food became dangerously scarce.

The problem was made worse by the fact that government officials were always under pressure to present Communism as perfect. The local officials would issue false reports about food production in order to impress their superiors. These reports would lead to unrealistic high expectations about the amount of grain that was going to be harvested. Then the officials higher up, going by the false reports, would take large amounts of grain from the peasant communes leaving little for the peasants to eat. All these factors combined to bring about the worst famine in the history of mankind. It is believed that from 1959 to 1961 at least 30 million people in China starved to death.

Many things I experienced during my college years helped shape my life, but none as much as what happened to me in my third year.

Sometime after I had started walking with the Lord, I began to notice that my asthma was improving. I even began to play sports again. I excelled in sports and began hoping for a glamorous future as a star athlete. Unlike drama or music, which was now mostly used for propaganda, sports remained relatively free from Communist control. I was particularly good at baseball and began to dream of the fame and money that could be gained with that kind of a career. I was being tempted along these lines when the Lord suddenly got my attention. During one of the games I severely injured my knee, and later had to return home to Shanghai for a time of recuperation.

Once again I was confined to my bedroom. However, as I spent time seeking the Lord, He spoke to me through His Word and showed me how I had been chasing the glory of this world instead of the glory of God. I repented and felt God's presence again in a way that seemed stronger than ever. I suddenly knew that He was calling me into the ministry. I trembled to think of it. "A preacher in an atheistic Communist country. Would I be able to withstand being persecuted? How would I be able to live with no salary, and what would I do in a country which had already closed most of its churches?" The temptation of this world was very strong, but God's love was stronger. Finally I yielded to the Lord and told Him that I would be whatever He wanted me to be.

However, somewhat like Moses, who spent 40 years in the wilderness as preparation, God would allow many years of suffering and trials in my life, in order to refine me for ministry. I still had too much of the world in me to be useful to Him. It took 30 years before the ministry to which I had been called that day finally became a reality.

Chapter 7

The Assignment

It was already late and no one except me seemed to be thinking about sleeping that night. The atmosphere in the room was still very tense. We had all just graduated, and the next day we would find out what jobs the government had assigned to us. In a free country a graduate chooses his own place of employment, we, however, were assigned our jobs by the government, and they were more or less for life. It was a crazy night for graduates all over China.

Lu, whose bed was near mine, was obviously feeling the strain. "How can you sleep?" He asked me with a curious look on his face. "Aren't you going out with us for a drink?"

I just smiled, "No thank you." I knew he wouldn't understand and I felt sorry for him.

"What, do you have nerves of steel? Aren't you worried?" he continued, lighting a cigarette for the first time in his life with shaking hands.

"Nah, I'm just tired." I replied. I turned over and pulled the covers over my head. I couldn't explain to him about the peace of God. At least not until all the frenzy had died down. Personally I was hoping to be able to return to Shanghai. It was still my favorite city and would always be home. However, I wasn't worried about it. I had prayed, and put my future in the Lord's hands. I trusted that He would direct my life according to His will. Everyone finally left the room and it got quiet. I closed my eyes and drifted off to sleep in the peace of the Lord.

I didn't know what to expect the next morning as I went to the meeting where the Communist official was to announce our assignments. I admit my heart beat a little faster as he stepped to the podium to read a list of our names and the particular jobs we were to be assigned to. My grades were good, but it was well known I was a Christian. "Would I be sent to some backwater village where I would wither away?" I wondered.

When he began, I couldn't believe my ears. My name was the first one on the list! I had been assigned to the prestigious Institute of Geology at the Chinese Academy of Sciences in

Beijing. I would be near my aunt and could attend her house church once again. What a relief! I decided I had to resign myself to living in Beijing. It seemed for me that all roads led to Beijing, and that it was clearly God's will that I return there. I was originally from the South, and I spoke the Shanghai and Cantonese dialects, and was familiar with its culture. But since God had repeatedly sent me to Beijing in northern China, I learned its culture and improved my Mandarin. This later proved very valuable in my ministry.

I started work for the Institute in 1961. For the next three years, my life and career followed a normal course. My job was typical of a field geologist and just as my friend Paul Li had predicted it was full of adventure. However, the life of an explorer can be quite rigorous. It's one thing to go camping for a weekend, and then return to your clean and comfortable home. But on geological expeditions we often spent 2 to 3 months camping out. And having grown up in the city I didn't have the same stamina as my colleagues from the country. However, God would use this also to train and equip me for my future ministry, which would require much the same type of rigorous travel and endurance of difficult living conditions.

We would hike to a location and set up our

base camp for the week or so that we worked in the area. Then everyday we would hike an average of 30 miles to and from different exploratory sites. On the way in we carried our equipment and supplies for the day in packs and on the way out we had the added weight of the rocks and fossils we had collected. We carried poles across our shoulders with packs hanging on both ends.

We faced many hardships from the environment as we traveled. We often passed through desert regions that were so hot that the sun burnt our bare skin to a crisp. If we were fortunate to find a desert spring, we would jump in clothes and all, bathing and drinking at the same time the cool refreshing water. One time we were hiking through a bamboo forest which had recently been cut, and small, sharp bamboo spikes were left sticking up from the ground. I was hurrying to keep up and accidentally stepped on one that went straight through my shoe. Blood spurt out, but I had to keep going. It was so painful that I limped along on the side of my foot, and continued walking every day for a month with my foot like that.

Sleeping at night during these expeditions, especially in peasant homes, was an experience all in itself. The bugs would declare all out war as soon as the sun went down. The mosquitoes would attack like fighter jets flying over and striking at will. On the floorboards where I usually slept, bed bugs rumbled along underneath me like tanks bent on destroying anything or anyone in their way. And guerilla warfare was carried out with zeal by a hidden army of man-eating fleas. In many peasant homes it was a step up for me from sleeping on the floor to be offered a coffin for my evening repose. Preparing a coffin early for an aging family member is a Chinese custom. It is actually comforting to the elderly to have their final resting-place constructed in advance. The coffins though served many purposes prior to their final destination, such as storing food, or as in my case, a guest bed.

On expeditions to the Tibetan Plateau, I traveled through areas where not only is clean drinking water in short supply, but finding even enough water suitable to bathe in, is difficult. At times I went for weeks without a bath. Tibetans however had no problem with this. They have a saying that "to take a bath will wash your fortune away". The old joke about Tibetans and their bathing habits is not far from true. It is said that they take three baths in their lifetime. The first when they are born, the second when they get married, and the third after they die.

When we would come down from the mountains on the Tibetan Plateau we were always extremely thirsty. We would stop at the first Tibetan tent we found and ask for some water to drink. Usually the Tibetan women were very warm and hospitable hostesses. The lady of the home would prepare tea for us. When she took out a bowl or cup for us to use it was usually quite dusty and dirty. But to solve that problem she would simply lift her skirt and wheel the bowl around several times on her knee. There was no thought of wasting precious water simply for cleaning purposes. Or if she really desired to show respect to her honored guests, she would stick out her tongue and clean the cup with a few good licks. But putting our delicacies aside we heartily drank down the tea, and it was actually quite delicious and maybe even a little "nutritious".

I always enjoyed however, being out in nature. Many times we were in remote places that were very beautiful. I would get alone and spend wonderful times worshiping God in the beauty of His creation. I always felt somehow nearer to God on the top of a mountain.

God had chosen for me a career in geology and He used it to shape my life and ministry in many ways. Even pitching tents in the wilderness served as a reminder to me that we are only pilgrims in this world passing through to the promise land much like the Israelites erecting the tabernacle in the desert. Like John the Baptist, life in the wilderness separated me from dependence on so much of what we consider "necessities" in life. It totally changed me to where I was no longer a spoiled "city boy", and was better prepared to be God's servant.

In 1965, things changed for many of us "intellectuals" who had been educated in the universities. Another government "movement" was initiated. This time it was to help "the privileged class of intellectuals understand the plight of the peasant farmers," by forcing us to work on a commune for a year. Also, there was widespread corruption among communist officials in the rural districts and the government hoped that our presence would help to curb it. They thought we wouldn't be as easily taken advantage of as were the peasants.

Needless to say there was a good deal of murmuring among my colleagues about having to leave their research for a whole year to go live and work in primitive conditions. It was easy to feel that way, but I tried to remember that I was no longer in charge of my life. I would not have chosen this path, but I trusted that my Heavenly Father had a plan for me and it was good. God taught me much during that year including a lot about farming, and it also served to make me stronger as I overcame the physical hardships.

The plan of the Communists was that "intellectuals" and peasants would share "four essentials": living together, eating together, working together and studying Mao's philosophy together. I was sent to a poverty stricken district in the province of Henan.

Sharing living quarters with the peasants challenged me in many ways. I stayed in several different homes during that year and each one was a unique experience. I remember one family offered me their kitchen to sleep in, along with their livestock. I shared my room with chickens, pigs, sheep, and dogs. Not only was it noisy, but it obviously didn't smell very good either. That winter I stayed with a family of seven. They were so poor that in order to stay warm at night they all had to sleep together fully clothed with only two quilts to share. Since they could not all fit under just two quilts one of the boys had to sleep with a neighboring family. One night however, he asked if he could share my "personal" quilt. I felt sorry for him so I said ok. Little did I know that this boy was a prime example of why the Chinese say, "When one gets many lice, one doesn't feel the itching."

He was covered with lice but never even seemed to scratch. I, however, soon felt the itching! I had nothing but cold water to wash with. And it was a long time before I was rid of those lice.

People in the West can hardly imagine the lack of variety that makes up the Chinese peasant's diet. In the area where I was located the only thing that grew well were sweet potatoes. A fresh baked sweet potato is delicious, but if you eat them day after day they begin to turn your stomach sour. Even worse they would only last a few months before they began to rot. So at harvest time we would preserve the majority by placing them out in the sun to be dried. These then became our major source of food the rest of the year. But each month that passed they turned progressively more moldy, soiled, and bitter. Thankfully we had food coupons from the government to supplement our diet, and could get rice, and flour. The peasants didn't have this privilege and so we shared with them by combining it with their course food.

There were no machines or even farm animals to help us with our work. But in China there is a never-ending supply of manpower. Every morning two or three of us would push a huge lever on a well pump round and round to supply water to irrigate the crops. I was always dizzy by the time we finished. We would also plow the land using sometimes as many as ten people to pull the plow. And the land would usually have to be cleared by hand before we could even begin our work. I experienced the backbreaking work of rice planting as well, with its constant bending over. I was in such poor shape that even old women and young girls put me to shame. The peasant women may look fragile, but they are really quite strong.

Every evening we were required to gather together to study Mao's philosophy from his books. We were supposed to study it privately every morning also, like a religious devotion, but I never did. I had taken my Bible with me and I would use the morning sessions to spend time with God. My personal devotions were the only spiritual encouragement that I had for that whole year. There were no other Christians in that area that I knew of. God was teaching me to stand with Him even if I was the only one.

Chapter 8

The Cultural Revolution

"In just a few hours," I was thinking, "I'll be back in Beijing, soaking in a hot bath." My year in rural Henan was finally over, and I was eager to get back to the city. I was craving good food once again and could already taste my aunt's mouth watering steamed dumplings stuffed with deliciously spiced meat. Also I couldn't wait to see her and my step-grandmother, and the other believers that met in her home. I had so much to share with them and was starving for Christian fellowship.

I hadn't been able to let them know that I was coming so there was no one to meet me at the station. I collected my bags and looked for transport to my aunt's home. Thirty minutes later I was knocking on her door. I had changed so much since I first came here from my parent's more luxurious home in Shanghai. This had now become the only place that I really thought of as home. I suppose it was because my parents and I could not share the most important thing in life, a personal relationship with Jesus Christ. But I was sure of a warm welcome in my aunt's home and of her joy in seeing me again.

My step-grandmother answered the door. I knew she was glad to see me, but she seemed to almost hesitate a moment before letting me in. I was so happy to be back, all I could do was talk on and on. I didn't even notice her reserved behavior. Then my aunt came into the room. I was startled to see that she had cut her hair. It was short, and hung limply about her head in a very plain and unattractive manner. Also she had a very grave look on her face and barely even returned my enthusiastic greeting.

"Is anything wrong?" I asked, suddenly feeling puzzled. "Is Uncle Gordon ok?"

My aunt shook her head. " No, everything is fine. We are all well. But I would like to have a talk with you Freddie." She motioned to my step-grandmother, who went out, leaving us alone in the room.

My mind was racing. "Why was my aunt acting so strange? Had she heard some rumor or false report about me? What could it be?" I couldn't think of anything that I had done to upset her.

Slowly and deliberately she began to relate to me everything that had happened to her since I last saw her a little over a year ago. As she spoke it was like a bad dream, and I wished I had only to wake up to discover it was not real. Things had changed so drastically in the year that I had been out in the country. She was a schoolteacher, and like most of her peers, she had been going through a period of forced "reeducation" by the government. As a result, she now claimed that all that she had believed about God and the Bible wasn't true, and that she had confessed her "crimes" to the government. She had voluntarily turned her Bible over to the officials and had stopped holding meetings at her home.

I sat there in silence. I heard her words, but my mind would not let me take in what she was saying. This was my spiritual mother. She had been teaching me about Jesus ever since I was four years old. I could discuss so many things with her that I couldn't even talk about with my own parents since they didn't understand my belief in Jesus. When I would visit my parents, and the subject would come up, my father would grow irate and sometimes he would bang his fist on the table and shout, " Get out of my house if you still believe in Jesus. You can't stay here!" My mother too had tried her own tactics to get me to abandon my faith. She would often tell me sternly, "Before I die and am cremated into ashes, you had better change your beliefs." Understandably, I depended very much on my aunt's encouragement in the faith. When she had finally finished talking I didn't know what to say. And I didn't want to be disrespectful, so I awkwardly made an excuse that I needed to leave and get ready for work the next day.

I wandered the streets for a long while in a daze. I couldn't understand what had happened to my aunt. She had remained faithful during so many other past trials. Even when Pastor Wang had been arrested and his church closed, she had continued to hold house church meetings at great personal risk. As I walked along, I began to notice many changes in Beijing. Old shop signs seemed to have either had the words crossed out with red paint, or had been broken in pieces. I noticed that all the women had their hair cut short like my aunt. And none of them wore skirts or high-heeled shoes. After being almost completely isolated in the country the last year, I hadn't realized the changes that had occurred. I was seeing some of the effects of what came to be known as the "Cultural Revolution".

Historians will say that the Cultural Revolution officially began in 1966. However, the changes leading up to it began several years before then. China had become, in actuality, a dictatorship under Chairman Mao. And as is common with dictators he felt his power threatened, especially by his "number two man". By this time also, relations between China and The Soviet Union had soured. Each side claimed that the other had betrayed true Communism. Mao accused the number two leader of being a reactionary and a Soviet sympathizer. He also began to develop a plan for removing all Communist party leaders who, he felt, were not completely loyal to him. To do this, Mao needed to assemble a new force faithful only to him and totally under his control. Much of the established communist party was loyal to his "number two man", so he turned to the youth of the country. But before they could be mobilized, an enemy had to be invented. For that he turned to the establishment. I was affected by this part of his plan when I was sent to the farm for "retraining" for a year. The intellectuals were part of the establishment that was being slowly but surely "demonized" by Mao.

The education profession was also targeted. My aunt had been affected by the effort to "retrain" all teachers in the philosophy of

Chairman Mao. The old order and way of thinking, including all religion, was now portrayed as the problem. Everyone must conform to the new way of thinking, and brainwashing was being used to accomplish this. They taught that Mao's philosophy was the source of inspiration for all good deeds. They contrived role models of certain individuals who were said to have lived the pure and selfless communist life. These were people who gave up everything for Communism. Under this pressure my aunt gave up her belief in Christ. She was deceived into thinking that people were inherently good and needed only to act accordingly. No longer did she believe in God or eternal life. She had been brainwashed to believe that it was only your life on earth that mattered and that in time Communism would create a paradise.

In 1966 things were in place for Mao to make his move. He began his revolution by declaring that Communism in China could only succeed if it rid itself once and for all of what he termed the "four olds". By this he meant "the old ideas", "the old culture", "the old customs", and "the old habits". And who do better at getting rid of the old, than the young. Schools were closed, and almost overnight high school and middle school students were mobilized. An army of young soldiers was hastily roused out of the worst of the rabble. They were known as the Red Guards. They responded with fanaticism to Mao's call that China's centuries old culture must be destroyed. For this reason it was called the Cultural Revolution, though in reality it was nothing more than fascist terrorism, and it was one of the blackest pages in China's history.

Young people throughout China, responding to Mao's call for revolution, were casting off the natural constraints of teachers and parents. The latter were suspected of harboring the old culture and values. They could be classified as enemies of the state based solely on the position in society that their ancestors had held. If for example their father or grandfather had been a landlord or a Capitalist, this was enough to condemn them no matter how faithful they had been to the Communist party. Their own children were now being encouraged by the Communists to inform on them. Students revolted in classrooms and beat their teachers for holding to "the old ways".

The Red Guards entered the houses of these newly deemed enemies and drug them out into the streets and beat them. They would ransack their homes, burn their books, and confiscate or destroy any items that they considered as belonging to "the four olds". They also entered shops and destroyed anything, including signs that reflected China's old culture or Western culture. Women were not allowed to wear skirts, high-heeled shoes, or makeup. If they went to beauty shops to get their hair fixed, they were dragged out into the streets and had it forcibly cut short.

Mao's ultimate intention of course was to remove the leaders of the Communist party that threatened him. He could now simply accuse them of being too highly influenced by the past and in need of "retraining". Then suddenly, and without warning a group of Red Guards would show up at their homes, and they would be either beaten to death, sent to a labor camp, or tortured and imprisoned. Mao was a diabolical master at using the sinful nature of men to his advantage and was able to successfully get rid of a number of his rivals in this way.

Slowly but surely I began to pick up my life again in Beijing since having left my job at the Academy of Sciences a year before. For a long time I had wanted to find a committed Christian women and get married. I began seeing again, a Christian woman I had met a year before leaving for the country. Her name was Liu and she was a student at the music conservatory, and played the piano beautifully. I had thought that she must be God's choice for me to marry since she was a Christian, came from a good Christian family, and we shared many of the same interests. Her mother and brother were very committed Christians, but she struggled in her faith. She was facing many pressures from her school. Her instructors wanted her to abandon her Christian beliefs, promising her that if she would, they would see that she got a position at China's Central Symphony Orchestra. Liu was very talented and loved her music very much. She struggled bitterly with the idea that as a Christian she would have to give up a wonderful career and even possibly suffer for her faith.

I had convinced myself that she would eventually make a full commitment to Christ no matter what. After all any one can struggle with something and still get the victory over it. We had begun to talk about marriage and make tentative preparations for it. However, after my return to Beijing and the outbreak of the Cultural Revolution all that changed.

Her father had been a high official with the Nationalist government, which had been in power before the Communists had taken over. He had fled to Hong Kong to save his life, but his family was still under suspicion due to his association with the Nationalists. My girlfriend's mother sensed that trouble was coming and had gone to Shanghai to get away. Shortly afterward Liu and I met with trouble and were subjected for the first time to the wrath of the Red Guards. I was taking her home one evening after we had gone to see a ballgame. We found the Red Guards waiting for us at her door. They brazenly followed us in and after being harshly interrogated we were led out of the room. One of Liu's brothers and I were locked up together in the kitchen. They locked Liu in the bathroom. For the next five hours the Red Guards completely ransacked the small apartment. They smashed all the precious glassware, turned over all the furniture and tossed all books and magazines outside. They even destroyed some perfume and make up they had found.

This event shook up Liu so much that she would have little to do with me (or any other non-conformist) afterward. I was a zealous believer, and she was not prepared to face the dangers that life with me was sure to include. But I had no hard feelings toward her. It is difficult to walk the straight and narrow way of the cross. Her mother and brothers still loved me however and wanted dearly for us to get back together. They were of course unsuccessful, but ironically enough, they were instrumental in leading me to the right person the

Lord did plan for me to marry. At the time, however, things were looking very bleak. I had lost the precious fellowship of my aunt, and now I had lost my girlfriend.

But I was determined to follow the Lord, and though it seemed a lonely road, God was getting ready to change all that.

Chapter 9

Oriole in a Cage

Liu had a brother named Ren who lived in the city of Tianjin. He had married a very distinguished woman known in society as Madam Pan. Prior to their marriage, Pan had served a one-year prison sentence for unjust "political reasons". Both Ren and Pan had been very much in favor of Liu and I marrying. They were both visiting in Beijing a couple of months after Liu and I had broken up, and I went to see them.

"I am so sorry about you and Liu," Pan said compassionately. "Tell me, what kind of girl would you like to marry?"

That wasn't hard for me to answer, I'd thought a lot about it since we'd broken up. "I know one thing for sure, she must be willing to suffer for Christ." I answered rather emphatically, somewhat surprised at my new resolve.

But nothing else was really important to me, no matter how difficult it would be to find someone like that.

Pan nodded thoughtfully. We both knew how hard it was to meet fellow believers these days. With the current climate in China, few dared to openly proclaim that they were Christians. But unknown to us, God would use the very words I had just spoken to produce a meeting between my future wife, and myself. My words, "willing to suffer for Christ" would be brought back to Pan's mind at just the right moment.

Pan was a very weak woman physically, and probably would have died during her year in prison except for a very special young Christian woman by the name of Dorothy Chang. Dorothy had been placed in the same cell with Pan and had helped her stay alive. Dorothy's father had been a well-known Christian leader in northern China before the Communists had come to power. He had set up a Christian newspaper, and a foundation that supported Chinese evangelists. However, he would not give his allegiance to Mao, or the state run church, and had been in and out of prison since 1955.

Dorothy had been a promising dental student. She also had a beautiful voice, and had been trained to sing in the opera. However one day she was suddenly arrested and taken away to a prison labor camp. The Communists thought they could use Dorothy to entrap her father, and tried to get her to sign a confession stating that her father was an American spy. They also demanded that Dorothy renounce her own belief in God. They even promised her a successful career if she would only sign the confession. But she wouldn't believe a word they said. She was already familiar with their deceptive ways and hated them for their cruel treatment of her father.

Several years went by with her continually refusing to sign the confession against her father. Her captors thought that a year or two in prison would break her spirit, and cause her to betray her father and deny God. But the experience proved otherwise. Dorothy had never fully surrendered her life to God, and for the first time she began to see her own sinfulness through this trial. The extreme hatred she felt for her captors was disturbing to her and exposed the sin in her she had never before admitted to. She was convicted when she thought of Christ's love and His willingness to forgive her, and knew she must forgive her enemies in the same way. One day she finally surrendered herself completely to Jesus and was wondrously born again. Not only did she experience His forgiveness, but also she received his power to forgive others. She became a light in the darkness and ministered to others in the prison.

God began to open many opportunities for her to bless others. Since she had some knowledge of medicine, she was put in charge of the medical care of the other prisoners. Since Pan was in her same cell she was able to give her special attention. And because of her position, she was able to acquire glucose and vitamin injections for Pan, which helped strengthen her.

Dorothy showed Pan the love of Christ, especially in sacrificial ways. Every Sunday as a special food the prisoners were given two white steamed buns. The rest of the week however, they were forced to eat a coarse bread made with leftover food scraps, such as the shells of sunflower seeds. Miraculously, Dorothy was able to digest the coarse bread, but many of the prisoners could not even eat it, including Pan. All the prisoners treasured the little white steamed buns so much that they would cut them up into as many pieces as possible, and eat a little of it every day. However Dorothy would always give her two little steamed buns to Pan so that she would at least have some food she could digest. She would then take Pan's coarse bread and eat it instead. Without Dorothy's food, Pan would never have survived.

One evening Dorothy and Pan were talking about what they would do if they got out of prison. Pan was still not a Christian at that time, but having been so moved by Dorothy's love she told her that when she got out of prison she would marry a Christian. Soon afterwards Pan was actually released, but neither of them knew when or if they would ever see each other again.

After Dorothy had served six years of hard labor in prison, her case was finally brought to trial. In China, a person could be sent to a prison labor camp indefinitely without ever receiving a sentence or a trial. Dorothy had never officially been charged with anything. When her case finally came to court the judge seemed surprised that there was so little that she had done wrong and yet she had been in prison doing hard labor for the last six years. He commuted her sentence to that of a night parolee. To Dorothy, this was wonderful. She still would have to work six days a week in forced labor, but every night and on Sundays she would be able to go home and be with her parents. The Communists had confiscated rooms in their large comfortable home, until finally they were left with only a bedroom and a kitchen. But to Dorothy, it didn't matter, because at least she would be home.

One Sunday, after her parole, she was boarding the bus across town. She glanced up and at the same moment, they saw each other. She couldn't believe it! It had been over five years since she had last seen her dear friend Pan. They hugged and cried in a joyful reunion. Dorothy explained how she was now a second class prisoner, meaning that she was able to go home in the evenings and on Sundays. Dorothy asked Pan if she was married yet and Pan replied, "Yes and I married a Christian." Then Pan asked Dorothy if she was married and Dorothy responded that she was still waiting and praying.

Pan then asked her, "What kind of man do you want?"

Dorothy replied, "I'm waiting for a Christian man who is willing to suffer for Christ."

To Pan, those words sounded very familiar. "Where have I heard that before?" she wondered. "Oh yes, Freddie Sun used that exact same phrase when he told me what kind of wife he wanted." Looking thoughtfully now at Dorothy, Pan smiled and said, "I think I may be able to help you out."

They soon had to part again, but only after exchanging addresses and promising to get together soon. Dorothy had been so glad to see Pan and to learn that she had married a Christian. She didn't even think about Pan's offer to help her find a husband. She thought that Pan was simply being kind. A couple of weeks later however, Pan surprised Dorothy when she came by her home to ask her if she would be willing to meet a Christian brother visiting from Beijing next Sunday. God had ordered the circumstances and was now about to bring Dorothy and I together for the first time. I can still remember the way I felt when Pan told me about Dorothy.

"Freddie, I've found the perfect girl for you." Pan announced joyously.

She and Ren had made a special trip all the way to Beijing to tell me about Dorothy. They wanted me to come to Tianjin the following Sunday to meet her.

"I was in prison with this girl." Pan continued. "She would not renounce God, or betray her father, so she suffered greatly. When we worked at the labor farm, she was given the worst job – collecting manure in buckets all day long."

I listened intently as Pan told me different stories about their time in prison together. I learned how loving this girl had been to Pan. When she finished, I eagerly agreed to come to Tianjin the following Sunday to meet her.

I spent the next week dreaming of this girl. I tried not to get my hopes up, realizing that probably nothing would come of it. But it was no use, I was too excited.

Sunday finally arrived. Pan had arranged for me to meet Dorothy in a coffee shop. I remember I was so surprised when I first saw her. I didn't expect her to look so beautiful after all the suffering I knew she had gone through. Her hair was very pretty, and her face had an appearance of sweetness and gracefulness. My heart was immediately stirred as I looked at her. Could this gentle, delicate creature have gone through so much for our Lord? A great tenderness for her filled my heart.

We visited together for a long time and before we left, we agreed to correspond. Later, when I wrote her I shared things about the Lord and my concern for the church in China. Amazingly Dorothy seemed to understand my ideas and would even challenge me by the things she said concerning her commitment to the Lord. I was soon spending as many Sundays as possible visiting her. A couple of times on Sunday she was even able to come visit me in Beijing.

One day when I was alone on a mountain-top during a geological field trip, I suddenly found myself shouting at the top of my lungs: "I – love – her!" I felt as though all the mountains echoed back with their approval and the flowers and the trees smilingly agreed. I realized then, that I was head over heels in love. Through prayer, I became convinced that God had brought us together and I soon told her so. But Dorothy, although she felt the same, would not be totally convinced until I had met her parents, which I had not yet done. She had very godly parents, and fully believed that God would give them peace about me if we were to marry. I was quite nervous the first time I went to meet them.

I brought some strawberries as a gift. I was so distracted that day, that as I carried them along, I didn't realize that they were pressing up against my shirt. Just before I went in I looked down at my shirt and saw with alarm, huge red stains. "Well that's just great." I thought. "Now I'll really make a good impression." But I needn't have worried. Dorothy's father, David Chang, was a thoroughly gracious man, and we hit it off immediately. He was so loving and accepting, and hoped that God might be giving him another son that would share his love for the Lord. All four of his sons had tragically denied the Lord. Dorothy was delighted at the response of her father. And oddly enough, Dorothy told me later, the strawberry stains only made her love me more.

It was soon decided that Dorothy and I would marry. She would still be a second class prisoner and have to live in Tianjin. I would not be allowed to change jobs and would have to continue to live in Beijing three hours away. We knew from the outset that I could be arrested at anytime, and that Dorothy could be forced back into confinement, but we were sure that for better or worse, God had brought us together.

Before we could legally get married we had to get certificates that proved we were single. The state security personnel department normally issued these. They approved me without a problem since I had a job, but Dorothy had to go through the courts since she was a night parolee from prison. Her certificate was finally issued however, and sent to the Institute of Geology where I worked. The head of security there soon showed up at my office. We had roomed together at one time, and so I knew him very well.

"I've got some bad news for you Freddie." He said solemnly.

I stared at him. "So it has finally come." I thought. I had no doubt what he was referring to. It was well known I was a Christian. These were terrible times. My heart skipped a beat. "Was I to be arrested today?" I waited for him to continue, expecting the worst.

"The girl that you are planning to marry is not what she seems. Has she told you that she is serving a prison term as a day laborer, and only let out in the evenings and on Sundays. She probably didn't want to tell you, until she had got you hooked."

Suddenly feeling very relieved; I thought to myself. "So that's it, he's talking about Dorothy. She's viewed as a common criminal, like a prostitute or thief, for simply not denying Jesus."

Forcing a smile, I tried to respond gently. "I know that she is a night parolee. I knew that before I even met her. She has told me every detail of why she is in prison, and others have confirmed it all." I paused for a moment, and then said looking straight at him. "She's really a very good person and I intend to marry her."

Totally unconvinced, my friend exclaimed, "Think what you are doing. This could affect your whole future. You know how things are right now. It's important to show that you are a good citizen of our great country. Don't you realize that you'll be under suspicion if you marry a person who our government has declared a criminal? I just don't want anything to happen to you."

I stood firm, and after repeated arguments he finally left. I believe he sincerely had been trying to warn me. I knew that it was dangerous to marry Dorothy, but I believed that God's grace was sufficient. He had showed me to marry her and had filled my heart with such love for her that I could not do otherwise. She had lost her freedom in this world for the sake of our Lord. I thought of her as so fragile with her gentle disposition and her sweet singing voice. To me she was like a beautiful singing bird locked up. I called her my oriole in a cage.

We were in the midst of the most difficult days of the Cultural Revolution. The Red Guards roamed the streets, viciously searching for victims. They had been to the Chang home many times. At first they came to torture David Chang and to ransack his home, but they had begun to tire of that and now just came to extort money. They were really just young kids wanting extra pocket change. The government had given them their authority, and they of course, abused it.

On October 24, 1967, the day we had chosen for our wedding, the Red Guards showed up again. I was getting ready to take Dorothy to get our marriage license when they arrived.

Dorothy's mother told us she would deal with it and told them to wait in the hall while she went to get some money. Her family always tried to keep a little money for the Red Guards. They would accept it greedily, then go on their way. Dorothy and I went down the stairs walking past them on our way out. They looked haughtily at us, making rude remarks as we passed. We had no church to be married in or wedding guests to stand and admire my beautiful bride as she passed by; instead we had the Red Guards. We headed for the police station, which was the usual place people went to be married. The ceremony was short. We filled out our marriage license, and paid the 20-cent fee. We were married. It was that simple.

When we returned home, Dorothy's family tried to make things special for us. They prepared a delicious feast for everyone with special foods which none of us had had for a long time. We spent the evening talking and laughing, enjoying the sanctuary of love and peace in the Chang home. I had felt so alone after my aunt had denied the Lord, but now God had given me a wife, and new Christian parents.

That evening after everyone had gone to bed, Dorothy lay in my embrace on our makeshift bed. For our bridal suite we had been given the kitchen. We had candles for light and laid some old boards together to form our bed. But we were so happy. Knowing how short our time together would be, helped us to savor every moment.

I whispered to my bride. "Now we are one. It was God's will that we should marry, and as long as we stay faithful to the Lord, we will be our own small church. Two lights burning every brighter in the Body of Christ. Let us dedicate our lives together to His glory."

Chapter 10

Monsters and Demons

I was running late that Monday morning to my office at the Institute of Geology. I had overslept after returning late the night before from Tianjin where I had spent the weekend with Dorothy. Nine months had passed since we were married and I visited her every chance I got. It was summer and though still early in the day, it was already quite hot. I hurried along, with that anxious feeling that I always had whenever I was made to stand out. These were troubling days, it was 1968 and the Cultural Revolution at this time was in full progress.

Stepping out of the bright sunlight I entered into the large main lobby of the geology building. Then suddenly I stopped cold. Forcibly blinking my eyes, trying to adjust to the dim indoor lighting, I stared dumbfounded at the walls in front of me. I couldn't believe what I was seeing, but it was true! My turn had finally come!

Huge posters caricaturizing me in a harsh and ridiculing, cartoon fashion, decorated the lobby of the Institute. In every direction that I looked my name was plastered next to long lists of crimes I was supposedly guilty of committing. In some of the cartoons, I was caricaturized as a Catholic priest, wearing a long, black robe and a rosary with a huge cross on it around my neck. The Communists never could seem to get the differences between Protestants and Catholics straight. On the posters bold dramatic words proclaimed: "FREDDIE SUN – COUNTER REVOLUTIONIST AND REACTIONARY CHRISTIAN."

Immediately guards surrounded me and placed me under house arrest. The Red Guards were then promptly dispatched to go ransack my apartment and look for any incriminating material they could find. Very quickly they discovered my diaries. These represented the last sixteen years of my life in which I had daily recorded all my thoughts, hopes, and dreams. For some time now I had been aware of the danger involved in keeping them. But I hadn't been able to give up the only means I had of expressing myself freely in such a restrictive society. So

I had compromised and gone through the diaries with a scissors cutting out all the names of my friends wherever they were mentioned. I made especially sure that all the believer's names were removed and house church locations could not be identified. In this way the only danger was to myself. However, the Communists were not easily deterred and they scrutinized my diaries with a fine-tooth comb. They were determined to find something to accuse me of. It was amazing what they would come up with. I will give just one example. In 1960, I had written that the Lord's return was near. At that time Chang Kai Shek of Taiwan was advocating a counterattack and an invasion of Mainland China. So the Red Guards concluded that since I had written that the "Lord" would soon return, I was without a doubt referring to "Chang Kai Shek". And this meant that I was obviously a Counter Revolutionary. In this same ridiculous way, they fabricated many groundless charges against me.

They took me to a small room and locked me in it for several days. They forced me to write endless "self-criticisms", which is a unique invention of the Communists. In these, a person is forced to write down all the ways that he or she has "sinned" against the state.

Then after that person has documented all his or her "crimes" on paper, they are held accountable for them.

The Communists were preparing a mass meeting in which several other recent victims and I would be formally denounced. I was taken to the large auditorium of the Institute. More than 600 employees crowded into the hall to view the latest enemy of the state. I was the youngest of those being denounced. Most others who had been accused up to this point had been high-ranking Communist officials who were said to be secretly inclined towards Capitalism. I was the only one charged with "being a Christian".

As I entered the large crowded hall fear suddenly seized me. "How will I stand up to the beatings and verbal attacks?" I wondered. "Will they kill me, and if so how?" I thought of how the Red Guards were known to toss their victims off of high buildings, if it didn't kill them they would be maimed for life.

As I was paraded to the front of the hall, the Red Guards forced me to bend over double at the waist and hold my arms high in the air, known as the "airplane" many victims of the Cultural Revolution were tortured in this way. Also I was required to keep my head down to give the appearance of one too ashamed to look up. They hung a board around my neck that stated my crime and placed a tall paper dunce style hat on my head. Shouts of "Down with Freddie Sun!" filled the air as I walked to the platform.

However, just as I got to the front of the great hall, the fear I had felt so strongly a minute before suddenly left me. I was reminded of the Scripture; "You will be brought before kings and governors and all on account of my name. Make up your mind not to worry beforehand how you will defend yourself. For I will give you words of wisdom, and none of your adversaries will be able to resist or contradict you." I began to sing softly to myself the old hymn; "Onward Christian Soldiers." As I sang, I was encouraged that God was standing with me in this trial. For the next three hours, I stayed bent over double while one after another of my colleagues got up and criticized me. One of my lab partners who was the director's wife, was extremely aggressive. In her loud shrieking voice she kept on declaring, over and over, what a horrible person I was.

I was even forced to denounce myself. They gave me a gong to beat and paraded me throughout the institute's compound forcing me to repeatedly shout aloud that I was a "Counter Revolutionary". Some of my colleagues hit me and spit upon me. Most of them however, were professionals like myself and didn't really have their hearts in what they were being forced to do by the Red Guards. Later however, none of them wanted anything more to do with me, and I was treated as if I had some kind of infectious disease. But I was encouraged when I thought of the Scripture that says that the Apostles "have been made as spectacles for the whole world to see".

Afterwards I was taken to an old warehouse that had been turned into a holding area for all enemies of the State. It was called the "Monsters and Demons Cabin". All who had been accused were kept here and forced to write their self-criticisms. There were roughly three different categories of people in this group. First there were the high-ranking Communist officials that had been deemed as enemies of the State for being "too capitalistic". Second were the intellectuals, who were mostly professors accused of "clinging to the old ways". Most of them had been my own teachers and were all well-known research fellows of the Chinese Academy of Sciences. And third were those like myself who were considered to be a threat for any number of reasons. A few of the latter had ties from years ago to the former Nationalist government.

We were forced to sleep on worn out mattresses laid on wooden boards with only a thin quilt to cover us. Many of the professors were devastated by what was happening to them. They had never experienced shame and abuse like this. Some were even contemplating suicide. All of our homes had been ransacked and our careers were now over.

A few days later I was moved from the "Monsters and Demons Cabin" to a more select group that had been chosen for in-depth brainwashing. This group was made up of all that at one time had been students overseas. We were suspected of being secret enemy agents. I was amazed at the ridiculousness of this charge in relation to myself. I couldn't understand how they could possibly believe that the CIA had approached me and asked me to spy for them when I was in the United States. I was only twelve years old at the time!

In there effort to indoctrinate us into Communism, we were forced to say confession every day before a huge portrait of Mao Tsetung. "Maoism" had become the new state religion in China, and Mao was the new "deity" we were supposed to worship. We had to sing songs to him every morning and loudly recite quotations from his little red book. At the end of the day we were required to continue writing

William Wang Quincey, my great-grandfather on my mother's side, he was the British General Gordon's adopted son.

The third from the left on the back row is my great-grandfather, William Wang Quincey.

I weighed 9½ pounds when I was born.

My grandfather, Thomas Wang, on my mother's die with his 5 grandsons in 1936. My brother Wally is carrying me.

My father Jui-Huang Sun and my mother Agnes Kuo-Hsieu Wang Sun.

My cousin, Tommy Wang, and I are not only cousins but also have been buddies since childhood.

My mother came to Wellesley College as a visiting scholar in 1948 and brought me along with her.

Me in 1954 when I graduated from high school. The house in the background is where I attended house church meetings with my aunt and other believers in 1960.

At the back door of my parents' home in Shanghai in 1955 where I was born again.

Christian classmates and I met secretly in this park called Temple of Heaven in 1956 when I briefly studies physics in Beijing.

From 1956 to 1961 I studied geology at Nanjing University. I continued to meet secretly with other believers on the campus and in the surrounding areas.

God chose a geologist career for me so that I would be trained in the wilderness and be prepared to be His missionary. This picture was taken in Guagdong Province in Southern China.

I lost my freedom for 10 years. From 1968 to 1978 I learned from God the lessons that He wanted to teach me in my own specially designed seminary.

After the "Cultural Revolution" was over I was released and restored. I was put in charge of a geological expedition to Tibet. This picture was taken in front of the Potala Palace, where the Dalai Lama used to live, in Lhasa, Tibet.

Pitching tents at 17,000 feet on the Tibetan plateau. The oxygen level is only 1/3 of that at a normal altitude.

We rode horses on the Tibetan plateau because no vehicles can maneuver in the wild, hilly terrain.

At the subtropical border between China and Nepal, at the southern slope of the Himalayas.

Our wedding day, October 24, 1967.

God blessed us with fraternal twins, Joseph and Daniel, in 1972.

In November 1978, I was released from prison and we were united as a family for the 1st time. Joseph has always been taller than Daniel, a testimony that God gave us back our miscarried child.

Dorothy and I visited my father in Shanghai after I was released from prison. I still had very short hair growing back from the shaved head I had been forced to have as a prisoner.

God promoted me so much that I was the interpreter for Deng Xiao-Ping, the number one man in China, at an international science convention in 1980.

In 1987 I revisited the United States after 37 years. Churches in North Carolina helped Dorothy and me to celebrate our 20th wedding anniversary.

"As for me and my house, we will serve the Lord." Our reunited family celebrates Christmas in 1993.

our self-criticisms. My circumstances were now very similar to those of my wife's. Neither of us had been formally charged with any crime, and yet we had both lost our freedom.

Later it was decided that we needed to be humiliated even more by doing hard manual labor all day in front of our former colleagues. At first I was ordered to clean toilets and pick-up the trash but later the Red Guards decided that I would be good at construction and assigned me to masonry work. I had to learn from the beginning how to lay bricks, but I was soon doing quite well at it. It was strange to be doing this kind of work now everyday at the same place where I had so recently been practicing my profession. However I knew that God was doing a work in me, and I was learning obedience through the things I was suffering.

Not only did I learn to lay bricks, but I also learned how to do plumbing, carpentry, and many other skills. My foreman liked me so much that he even suggested that if I ever get the opportunity, I should quit geology and become a contractor. I saw first hand all that went into a building and became so accomplished that I eventually was allowed to lay the cornerstone brick. This is the most important brick in the whole building. If it is not placed correctly the other bricks will not be even. Jesus compared himself to the cornerstone for the Church. Everything in our lives depends on Him.

God gave me the physical strength I needed to do hard labor. At times I had to carry up to 200 pounds. Even though I had worked in the field as a geologist and on the farm for a year, I had never been accustomed to doing this much strenuous work. But it seemed as if God made me like Samson during those years. I had to do things that many times seemed beyond my ability to endure.

One winter the sewer backed up and the Red Guards came and got me in the middle of the night to clean it out. I was ordered to put on rubber clothing and gloves and to get down into the sewer and dredge it. The sewage was backed up so high that I had to get completely in and clear it with a bamboo rod. Soon my hands felt frozen and I was covered with slime. It took me two hours to finish and afterwards I was exhausted. For several weeks afterwards and many baths later, I still couldn't get the horrible smell off of me.

In the summers we were given equally unpleasant tasks. We were forced to enter the boilers and chip off the coal deposits that had formed on the inside. Not only was the sound of the hammer hitting on the inside of the boiler deafening, but it was so stifling hot inside, we could only stand it for short periods of time, before getting back out. Most of the others I worked with were professors, who were older, and couldn't handle such hard labor. So I often did not only my work, but also theirs to spare them.

I was forced to perform slave labor for five years. God was using it to stretch me and cause me to grow in Him. He had many things to teach me about obedience and humility. There was more breaking that He wanted to do in my life. Though I was more than ready to graduate, this was only the beginning of my special Seminary.

Chapter 11

Twins

The Bible says, "every good and perfect gift comes from the Father above." God's gifts encourage us, and are a reminder of His love for us as we face the many trials of life. God had graciously given me a wife, but now, just a little less than a year after we were married, and I had lost my freedom and was seldom allowed to visit her. Though this new trial seemed at times unbearable, I had only to look at Dorothy to be reminded of God's love for me. She was a gift from God, and I knew I had to trust Him to arrange our times together.

"Hey you two over there, hurry up with that concrete block!" the Red Guard supervising our work, shouted impatiently. "You're working too slow!" he began scolding us. "It's people like you that are holding back the progress of our great country!"

I looked over at Li and knew that he wouldn't be able to hold out much longer. He was even weaker than I was and the concrete block we had been carrying was so heavy and bulky that we could no longer manage it.

The guard had gone on but would be back soon, we had to keep trying to carry it. I knew that we'd be in trouble if we dropped it, but we'd be in worse trouble if we didn't fill our work quota for the day.

We bent over to lift it up and had just managed to get it off the ground when suddenly Li let go of his end. Grasping frantically but unable to keep hold of the full weight of the block, it jerked from my hands and fell to the ground, smashing my foot.

Immediately Li was at my side. "Oh Freddie, I'm so sorry," he sobbed. "I just couldn't carry it any more, I've never done any of this kind of work before."

I forced a smile, fighting back the throbbing pain in my foot. Li was older than I was, and very frail. He had been a scholar his whole adult life. It was no wonder he couldn't carry heavy concrete blocks.

A few minutes later our guard was back. He scowled at me when I told him what happened and how much my foot was hurting. He gave me permission however to bicycle to the hospital and have it looked at. That was some ride! I had to pedal with one foot the whole way there. After I was X-rayed, the doctor told me that I had fractured a bone, and shouldn't do anymore hard labor for at least three months.

The Red Guards decided that I should use the time to write more self-criticisms. But I had a different idea. "Why couldn't I be allowed to go see Dorothy?" I thought.

I knew I just needed to trust God to help me. So I approached the military commander in charge of the prisoners at the Institute and gave him my request. Amazingly enough, he agreed, but only under the following circumstances: I was to continue writing my self-criticisms every day, and report periodically to the local police station in Tianjin. Also I had to be accompanied by two Red Guards on the way there. And I wasn't allowed to go anywhere or visit anyone other than the police station. But none of that mattered to me because now every evening after seven o'clock, and all day on Sundays, Dorothy and I would be together.

Those three months were wonderful, it was like a honeymoon for Dorothy and I. And I had many precious hours of fellowship with my father-in-law, David Chang. I even learned how to cook from my mother-in-law. She taught me how to make foods such as dumplings, steamed bread, and noodles the way they make them in northern China. By now I had totally adopted the ways and culture of the Northern Chinese.

During this time Dorothy got pregnant. We had been praying for a child we could love, and train-up in the faith and were overjoyed at the news.

However, not long afterwards Dorothy had a miscarriage. Her work in the prison was most likely responsible for causing it. She worked in a factory that made window and door hinges. Since she was a Christian, the prison officials trusted her and gave her the job of sealing the boxes after she had verified that they each had the correct number of hinges. Once they were full, these boxes weighed over 100 lbs. After closing the box, she had to lift it and carry it to the shipping area. She carried over 20 boxes per day. Under these circumstances, it was no wonder that she lost the baby.

The three months were soon up and I had to return to forced labor in Beijing. Dorothy was very brave at our parting, but I knew that she felt just as bad as I did. I was leaving a part of my heart in Tianjin, and as I spoke I had to fight back the tears.

"Please take care of yourself," I pleaded with her. "I know it's hard, but we have to trust

God that somehow He will enable us to endure these trials."

For the next two years we both prayed continually for God's help. We wanted so much to be able to see one another again, and hoped for the day we would both be free from prison. We also prayed that He would give us another child. Occasionally I was able to get permission to go visit Dorothy. During the few traditional holidays, including the Chinese New Year, the Red Guards were actually lenient enough to grant me leave. In this way we were able to see each other about three or four times a year.

Two years after losing the baby, we found out that Dorothy was pregnant again. In her seventh month, the doctor told her that she would have twins. This would be joyful news for any parents, but particularly for Chinese parents. The government was already tightening its restriction of only one child per family. And since we were both considered enemies of the State we certainly wouldn't have been allowed more than one child.

Amazingly enough, I was given the customary fifty days leave to be with Dorothy during and after her time to give birth. She was still living with her parents and we were at their home when her labor pains began. The hospital was a mile away and there was no car or any other means of transportation available. The only way to get there was to walk. So we trudged along slowly, resting often as we went because of her labor pains. When we finally got there, Dorothy was ushered immediately into the delivery room, and I went and sat down in the waiting room.

Twenty-six hours later a nurse came into the room, her face beaming. "Mr. Sun," she said, "you have two healthy boys."

I was ecstatic! For in the Chinese culture, to have a son is a great sign of blessing on a person's life. And two at once is about as good as it gets. We have a saying that, "twice the happiness has arrived!"

I ran all the way home to tell Dorothy's parents. They rejoiced when they heard the news. In fact, it was such a novelty that just about everyone shared in the excitement. Not only the people at the hospital shared our excitement, even the police authorities from Dorothy's prison gave us hardy congratulations.

The most amazing thing about our twin boys was that they were nothing alike. At their birth Joseph was hairy like Esau but Daniel was without hair like Jacob. Also Joseph looked like Dorothy, while Daniel looked like me. And even though Joseph was born only seven minutes before Daniel, he was much larger. While growing up Joseph always looked two years older than Daniel, and remained half a head taller. It was clear to us that God had answered our prayers and miraculously given us back the child we had lost two years earlier, while blessing us with a second one at the same time.

I spent the next seven weeks getting a full dose of motherhood. Dorothy and her parents had been relocated to a smaller apartment, with only two rooms. We had one room, while Dorothy's parents and her sister shared the other. Our room was only about 120 square feet. We had just enough room for our bed, the baby bed, and a small stove. The boys shared the baby bed, each sleeping at opposite ends. I took the night shift caring for the boys. Dorothy, whose health was very unstable at this time, had a lady come in to help her care for them during the day.

Trying to keep them both fed and in clean diapers every night was a real challenge for me. It was always hard to remember which one I had fed last. Daniel, who's shorter than Joseph, to this day still jokingly blames me for it, saying that I fed Joseph more than him when he was a baby. I learned that being a mother was much harder than I realized. But I treasured that time, and it was all too soon before I had to return to Beijing. We were blessed to have Dorothy's parents there to help. She had to return to the day prison three months after the boys were born, and her mother did most of the caring for the boys after that.

The next two years passed by without incident. During this time I had become classified as a "less dangerous" enemy of the State. However, I was still only able to visit my family three or four times a year. I had been allowed to return to my apartment in Beijing, and though I was still doing some hard labor, I was given a little work in the labs again.

One of the greatest blessings however, was that God had given me a Bible once again. The Red Guards had confiscated mine years earlier when they ransacked my home. I happened to be visiting my uncle's home nearby. He had given me a key to his house before he was sent to the countryside to be "re-educated" as there was no one else living there to look after it. He had an incredible number of books that had somehow escaped the attention of the Red Guards. My guess is that since most of them were in English, (my Uncle spoke English and had been a journalist with Reuters News Agency) the Red Guards not knowing what they were, simply ignored them.

My Uncle was not a believer, but had always prayed whenever he was in trouble and even acknowledged that "only Christianity could save China". Even so, as I looked through his collection I was surprised to come across some Christian books. I started combing through them eagerly holding my breath, and hoping that just maybe...then suddenly my eyes fell upon it and my heart leaped for joy. It was a beautiful old English Bible.

I left his home that day elated. God had blessed me with one of the relatively few Bibles left in China. After that, it didn't seem as lonely in the evenings, as I spent much of my time reading and meditating on God's Word.

However, not long afterwards, my evenings alone came to an end. Dorothy started having kidney trouble and was too sick to care for the boys. They were only two years old at the time, so we decided that it would be best for them to come live with me in Beijing. I would hire a babysitter during the day. It wasn't ideal, but Dorothy was so sick that we feared for her life.

At first I kept the boys with me at night, and at the babysitters during the day. But soon I found it too difficult taking them back and forth each morning and evening. So I decided they would stay with the babysitter all week and come home only on Sundays. I still saw them every evening, and this way it was much better for all of us.

God's good and perfect gifts had come to me once again in the midst of trials. He had blessed me with a sweet godly wife and two beautiful children, while suffering persecution for His sake. In the coming days however, I would receive even greater gifts from God, the fruit of His Spirit. These, I learned, come only through trials, persecution, and death to self.

Chapter 12

Arrested

I turned over once again on the hard prison bed. I was too miserable and wide-awake by now to try to sleep. I could not stop my mind from racing over all the events of the last day and a half. Every hour I would hear the doors of the cell scrape open, as the guards peered in at us to take another head count. The dark, dank walls of the prison cell seemed to be closing in on me. I had been tossing and turning all night. In desperation I cried out to God, "Lord, I don't know what's happening or why I've been arrested, but I just need to know that you are here with me."

It seemed impossible that only less than 18 hours ago, I had been in my apartment getting dressed, and preparing to go pick up my boys for a day at the zoo. Joseph and Daniel like most toddlers had a strong fascination for animals. They had squealed with delight when I announced that I would take them to the zoo the next day, which was Sunday.

"Lions and monkeys" Joseph called out excitedly, causing Daniel to begin shouting at the top of his lungs, "panda, panda." They already had their favorite animals too.

At 7:00 am in the morning as I was still getting dressed, I heard a knock at the door. I went to open it, wondering who it could be this early on Sunday morning. I recognized immediately the Head of Security at the institute where I worked and the Communist Party Secretary. I looked at them in surprise.

The Head of Security was the first to speak and with a bland voice said simply, "The leader would like to interview you."

Good, I thought, finally they're ready to admit that I was accused unfairly in 1968 of being an enemy of the State. It was now 1974, and I had been doing hard labor for six years. I had been told that at some point the leader of our institute would review my case. I thought the time had at last come, and I would now be allowed to return full-time to my research work. Restrictions had been easing slowly for some time, so I had good reason to hope. Expecting to be coming right back, and as a free man, I didn't even close my window or turn off my light.

We stepped out of the building and walked to where a jeep awaited us. Four tall, muscular men were waiting on the curb. Two of them got into the front seat, and the other two got into the back seat on either side of me. The Head of Security and his cohort waved us on and we sped off. From where I lived the institute was to the North. But I noticed that we were heading south, and I began to get a sick feeling in my stomach that something was wrong. These men, it occurred to me, might be plainclothes policemen. As soon as we were outside the city limits of Beijing they stopped the jeep.

One of the men in the front turned to me and said, "You are under arrest!"

I sat stunned, watching in disbelief as all four men got out and hurriedly changed back into their official police uniforms. Then, just as quickly as though it had all been rehearsed, they jumped back in and we sped off down the road.

I didn't understand until later why they had driven me out of Beijing before arresting me. But it turned out they were from the police headquarters of Tianjin, my wife's hometown, and it was illegal for them to arrest a resident of Beijing in the city limits. So careful to follow the letter of the law, they drove me outside the city, to make the arrest.

At the prison officials office I found out that I was suspected of being a "rebellious and reactionary church leader". They believed that I, along with my father-in-law, had helped to organize an illegal house church movement. Also an acquaintance of my in-laws had been arrested for committing adultery. He had told the police, under torture, about some idle remarks I had made to him once about the Communists in Beijing. This was still the Cultural Revolution, and everyone in the government was suspicious. The main charge however, was that I was leading a rebellion and conspiring with other Christians against the government. They even drug up my old diaries again, convinced that they had the proof, in black and white. In a true democratic society, where people have civil rights, such things as, innocent, idle remarks about the government, fellowshipping with your father-in-law, or writing your thoughts in a diary, would never be a reason to arrest someone. But China in 1974, was anything but democratic.

All day Sunday I had been interrogated. The police officials were relentless. Over and over they shouted and slapped the table. "Tell us who else is involved with you in these crimes."

They tried their hardest to intimidate me, but all I could think about were my two boys back in Beijing, waiting to go to the zoo.

"Listen", I said, hoping for at least a spark of humanity among them, "I have two babies in Beijing who are waiting for me to pick them up. The baby sitter will not know what to do with them. Will someone please notify my wife to pick them up."

"Don't worry," one of the officials barked at me impatiently, "we'll take care of it."

However, later I found out that they lied, and never even told my wife that I had been arrested. The babysitter had begun to get worried when I didn't show up that Sunday, or in the evenings the following week, as I was accustomed to doing. After two weeks went by and I still hadn't come by to visit or to pay her, she realized that something was definitely wrong. She got word to Dorothy, who immediately sent her sister to Beijing to pick up the boys. She had no idea what had happened to me, and wouldn't even find out for an entire year that I was now on the men's side of the exact same prison where she was.

After many long hours of intense interrogation, they finally gave up, and led me to the prison cell I was now in. I knew in my heart that I should be joyful for being persecuted for Jesus. But I was struggling, and didn't feel joyful. I began questioning God why He had allowed this to happen to me. "Hadn't Dorothy and I suffered enough already? Who would take care of our boys? Would the State take them away from us?" This was only making me feel worse.

But as the night turned into early morning, the Holy Spirit began gently and patiently to work in my heart and I knew that I must begin to praise God, even here. As I began to thank and praise Him, I felt His peace descending. I heard His still small voice telling me that, as His servant, I would have to undergo the fiery trials of prison, but after I had learned many lessons, He would deliver me in not more than five years.

God had heard me, and had spoken to me. He had promised to deliver me. Suddenly all that mattered to me anymore was that He was with me in this dark and evil place. His comforting love surrounded me.

I turned over once again, but this time fell into a deep, peaceful sleep.

Chapter 13

Interrogated

The next morning I awoke to the familiar sound of the guard opening my cell door. I had only slept a few hours, but felt remarkably refreshed as though I had slept all night.

"Get up 390, breakfast!" the guard barked, addressing me by my new number.

I sat up and mumbled a thank you. I could hardly see what I was eating, and it tasted as bad as it smelled. But I hadn't eaten at all the day before, so I quickly wolfed it down. I looked around blearily at the dark corners of my cell. They had taken away my glasses so that I wouldn't break the lenses and slash my wrists. I was almost blind without them. Only a 25-watt bulb illuminated the room.

Half an hour later, the door opened again. It was the same guard, and without any explanation he uttered simply, "Follow me!"

For a brief moment I forgot everything the Lord had spoken to me the night before, and began to think that just maybe they were going to let me out. However, as it turned out, they were only leading me back to the interrogation room. And for the next month I under went intensive interrogation everyday. It would start in the morning, and go until evening. Sometimes they would continue far into the night. Manipulating, probing, threatening, all to try to draw out from me what I knew about the house church movement.

The night sessions were the worst. They would keep me awake for hours on end, shining a blinding light in my face. I couldn't see them as they questioned me, and it created a very disorienting affect. I was past the point of exhaustion, but the officials wouldn't let up.

"So let's go over again what we already know." The official continued, in a manipulative way. "You said earlier that you had organized house churches both here and in Beijing, through contacts given to you by your father-in-law, David Chang."

"No, No, I didn't say that," I replied wearily. My brain was beginning to feel like mush. I knew I hadn't told them anything, but with my head swimming the way it was, I was starting to have trouble remembering what I had or hadn't said. I was sure however, that I hadn't said anything to incriminate my wife or father-in-law. They were skillfully trying to get me to slip up and confess something that they could use against us. I knew that David could be sent back to prison, and that Dorothy would lose her night parolee privileges if I even mentioned them. What I didn't know was that Dorothy's father had already been arrested just shortly after I had. However, they had not held him long because he had a bad heart, and the Communists had feared that he might die in prison.

Between the interrogations I would be locked in my cell, once again writing endless self-criticisms. At least I had been given back my glasses, after I insisted that I couldn't write without them. One would think by this point, that I wouldn't have anything left to criticize myself about. But I had developed a certain method for writing the self-criticisms. I would start off by telling about my great-grandfather, and all of his exploits. I was as wordy as possible, writing pages and pages of family history. I would even confess that I had been spoiled as a boy, how I had loved having servants, and all the wealth of the "bourgeoisie" life. Sometimes I would write about my trip to the US, and the ice cream, and movies. I wrote volumes of material, and never incriminated anyone. Though as much as I wrote, they were still never satisfied.

"We know that you have been involved with the counter-revolutionary groups. So just tell us who and where, and we will let you go. You will get back your position as research assistant." The official had said.

They were lying of course, and even if I had been willing to tell them, they would only have used it against me. I had ceased to trust the Communists many years ago and this latest treatment had done little to restore my confidence in them. So I used a common tactic in avoiding the questions of my interrogator. I would confess things that people who were now dead had told me or done. That way no one could be incriminated who was alive.

At times, the official and I were like two boxers circling each other around the ring. Butting heads every few minutes. I was determined however, not to let him get the better of me.

"Come on man, tell me about the house churches!" He had shouted, after hours of getting nowhere.

"It is a religious not a political matter." I had wearily persisted. "All we do is read the

Bible and talk about Jesus. The Christian Church began with house churches, and we are not to "forsake gathering together". Besides, our own constitution guarantees religious freedom.

After more than a month of trying unsuccessfully to intimidate me in this way, they decided to change their approach. They put me in a cell with a medical doctor named Wang. He was in prison for having committed adultery. At that time it was considered a crime, and a person could actually be sent to prison for it. It was a minor crime however, and Wang would get out much quicker if he cooperated with the Communists. Unknown to me, he had been told he was getting ready to be placed with a "big fish". He was supposed to get information out of me and report it back to them.

Their idea however, backfired, and Dr. Wang took a liking to me. Instead of reporting on me, he took me under his wing and taught me all the ropes of the prison. I learned such things as, which guards could be trusted, and which could not. We had many good, long conversations. He even told me that the Communists had wanted him to inform on me, but that he was going to try to protect me.

For over six months I was in a cell with just Dr. Wang. We were better off than most of the others, who were crammed in with as many as ten others to the same size cell. I was being treated better than those who were convicted criminals, such as murderers or thieves. The Communists were hoping that I would eventually trust them and tell them what they wanted to know.

The guards used a large ladle to serve us our food. It didn't seem to matter to them that there were only two people in our cell, they still dished out a full ladle each time. So for the first six months, the amount of food we received was actually more than we needed. But we ate it all so that the guards wouldn't realize that it was too much food and start giving us less. Also the meals were mostly grains, containing very few vegetables, or meat, so we were concerned about getting proper nutrition. We wouldn't even pick out the fish bones for example, but chew them up to get the calcium. We ate so much food that we actually began to gain weight. We even tried to exercise to take some of it off, but it was hard to do, in a cell only 120 square feet in area.

For a short time the police even quit inter-rogating me and temporarily suspended my case so that they could travel to the scenes of my crimes and gather more information. I suspect that the police just wanted to get out and travel, especially to Beijing, but at least they left me alone for a while.

Not long afterward, however, the prison officials decided to change tactics again. They weren't getting the information they desired, neither from Dr. Wang, nor from the investigations of my background. So the interrogations started up again, and this time with increased threats to my life.

"Mister, you are so stubborn! You're going to take your granite head with you to see your God!" The official shouted. He was using one of Chairman Mao's favorite expressions. It meant that the person was going to be shot. Political prisoners were often intimidated in this way. And many would confess to the false accusations against them, even if it meant making up lies about others in order to save their own lives.

Threatening me, however, only seemed to make me more belligerent. Something would rise up inside of me, and I would boldly answer back, " You have no right to kill me! I'm not a murderer, or thief, or an arsonist! I've done nothing for which you could legally put me to death!"

It had now been more than half a year and still they had no new information or evidence against me. Long grueling sessions of interrogation had not worked. Placing me in a cell with only Dr. Wang had not worked. Even threatening me with death wasn't getting them anywhere. In their minds, the only thing left to do was subject me to the worst conditions the prison had to offer. So they came and got me out of the cell with Dr. Wang and told me I was moving.

Chapter 14

The Seminary

The heavy steel door to the cell slammed shut behind me. I stood for a long moment staring, aghast at the new grim surroundings. Sixteen men sat on benches that lined the two walls. The cell, the same size as the one I had just left, seemed even smaller with so many men in it. Above their heads dangled the ubiquitous 25-watt light bulb. The strong odor immediately told me, that the bucket in the far corner was the toilet. Next to it was another bucket, which I later learned was our washing water.

The men looked me over with interest. I was a diversion in the midst of their uninterrupted tedium. It was the usual custom when a new prisoner was brought to the cell, for the other prisoners to ask him if he wanted "wind or rain". If he responded "wind" they would promptly place a large quilt over him, and punch him until he fell. If he said "rain", they would place the quilt over him just the same, only kick him instead. The guards would order the prisoners to do this, hoping to make the new prisoners more submissive. God protected me, however. The guard did not order the others to beat me. Maybe since I had already been in the prison for over six months, he didn't think of me as a new prisoner. But whether he forgot or was just being lenient, I didn't care, all I know is that I was grateful for God's protection.

A moment later I was bombarded with questions from all sides. I was the only thing new that had happened lately and was now the center of their undivided attention.

"What's your name?" What did you do?" How long have you been in here?"

"Where are you from?"

It was quickly apparent that I was somewhat of a greenhorn in comparison to most of the others. Though a few were political prisoners like myself, the majority, it seemed were murderers, thieves, or pickpockets. They took delight in giving me advice, telling me things like: never confess to anything you did even if there were witnesses, and only talk about the most minor aspect of your crime. Most of the advice was not new to me, but I thanked them just the same, realizing that this was helping me to make friends.

I had my set place among the hard benches along the wall, where we were required to sit in an upright position the entire day. But after just a few hours my back would begin to ache terribly. Sitting there all day among the stench of unwashed bodies, and human waste, made for long, miserable days.

We were not allowed to talk, but were supposed to fill our days studying Mao's little red book. However, most of my cellmates weren't exactly the studious type, and preferred to spend their time reminiscing about their lives of crime on the outside. They would take the precaution of posting a sentry at the door in case the guards were coming. Since I couldn't ever hear the guards coming, I once asked one of the men posted by the door how he could hear them coming?

"I don't use my ears", he replied with a grin, "I use my nose!"

At first I thought that he was just making a cutting remark, until he explained that the guards who were allowed to smoke (unlike the inmates) always smelled strongly of tobacco.

I had never been around criminals before, and the stories they told caused my hair to stand on end. I was learning just how base a man can become apart from Christ. I remember one short, swarthy fellow telling us why he was there.

"You see, I was in a gang," he began, "and one of the rival gangs had this girl who really, really liked me. I mean she wouldn't leave me alone. But I didn't like her, you see. So she got some of her gang members to give me a working over one night. And you know I didn't like that, see. And so I invited her over to my house, like for dinner, and I took my hands and placed them around her neck, like this." And with that he suddenly paused and holding out his huge hands he began looking around at those of us closest to him. My eyes widened as he fixed on me. Then suddenly catching himself, he looked down at the floor, muttering solemnly with an oath. "And that was the end of her." I made a note to myself not to annoy him, especially since he slept right beside me.

Then just when I thought I had heard enough, another one would start up, trying his best to top the other. "That's nothing, let me tell you what I did…."

And on it went. Each story more gruesome than the one before it. And always using the most vulgar language to describe the filth of their lives.

Mealtimes had also taken a downturn. It was good that I had put on a little extra weight when I was with Dr. Wang, because I was now on the reducing plan. The guards didn't seem to care that our cell had sixteen men in it, and served us only a little more than Dr. Wang and I had received for just the two of us.

Nights were even worse than the days. Sleeping was just about impossible. For a bed, we had long planks that were kept underneath our benches during the day. And every evening we pulled them out and placed them between the benches to form a group bed. We had to lay in rows packed together like sardines. It was so tight we couldn't even lie on our backs. The stench of body odor and human waste would become overpowering at night in the stuffy little cell. The light bulb stayed on all night, and every hour the guards opened the door to check on us. It was all I could do just to lie there, and pray for morning.

At times we would get new prisoners in the cell. Often this was to replace others who had been taken out to await their execution. After a prisoner received a death sentence they would remove him to a special cell. They did this to protect the other prisoners, because often the condemned men became violent. The officials treated them with extra care, greatly concerned with keeping them alive until the execution. They even offered them their favorite meal on their final day. It was hard to imagine that anyone could have an appetite at that time.

From our prison cell window we were able to see the executions take place. We would watch as the guards often had to half carry terrified men to their deaths. Their faces were deathly pale, they often wet their pants, and sweat poured off of them. They were terrified not knowing what awaited them on the other side. Every unbeliever has some fear of death, a deep conviction in his heart that judgement will follow. I was struck by how different it was for the believer. Watching these scenes from the prison cell window gave me a deeper understanding of " how wide and long and deep is the love of Jesus Christ". I knew in my heart that I was no different from those being executed. I too was a sinner, and deserved eternal death. However, Jesus had taken my place forever on the execution block. Christians are the only ones in the world who do not have to be afraid of death.

On Sundays we were allowed to engage in different activities, such as playing chess or mending our clothes. We became quite industrious in supplying what we needed for these times. I learned how to make chess pieces from porridge, needles from toothbrushes, and thread from fibers.

Sundays were also the day we got special food as on festival days. In our boredom, much time was spent speculating on what we might eat that day. We could see the kitchen from our window, and had noticed that whenever smoke came out of a certain chimney, it was usually something good, maybe even meat.

One Sunday we had a rather humorous episode occur. We had enjoyed a breakfast that morning of tasty garlic noodles, and it being our "free day", were spending time much as we did on any Sunday. Some were sewing, others were playing chess, and I was giving haircuts to my cellmates.

Suddenly the door opened, and a guard we didn't recognize shoved in a bowl of delicious looking meat dumplings. We all stared in amazement. We normally only received meat dumplings on the Chinese New Year. There were only six of us in this particular cell at that time. We were often juggled around to keep from forming close relationships with each other. They had given us 36 dumplings. Not only was this an unusually special treat, but an enormously generous portion. We were of course, always hungry, and quickly grabbed up the bowl and each downed our six. We were still licking our fingers, smacking our lips, and expressing unusually congenial thoughts about our captors, when the cell door opened again. It was the same guard.

"Where are those dumplings?" he demanded.

Looking at him a little startled, I replied, "We just finished them, they were delicious, thank you."

He scowled back at me in disgust and slammed the door. A moment later, he came back followed by our regular guard, and opening the door, pointed in at me. Then he slammed the door again and they were gone. Next, our guard returned alone and opening the door, he grabbed the hair clippers, and gruffly ordered, "Get rid of your hair at once!"

I was stunned. Normally a prisoner was forced to shave his head only when he first entered the prison, as a form of humiliation. All the other prisoners in my cell had had their heads shaved in the beginning, but as it grew out I would trim it for them to keep it neat. However, I hadn't been subjected to this form of humiliation upon my arrival and couldn't understand why all of the sudden I was treated this way. It took a while to figure out what had happened, but eventually all the pieces of the puzzle fell in place.

In our prison there were a number of former high-ranking Communist officials that had been interred since the beginning of the Cultural Revolution. They had always received better treatment than the rest of us. They had not been forced to shave their heads, received better food, and had more comfortable quarters. The guard that had brought us the dumplings was the prison cook. As he was rushing the hot dumplings to some of the more "elite" prisoners, he mistook me for a high-ranking Communist official. Apparently because I still had my hair. Our guard, however, made sure that mistake would never happen again.

One day the guards brought an unusual prisoner to our cell.

"Get in there, and keep quiet, we've had enough trouble out of you!" a guard barked as they shoved the prisoner in and quickly slammed the door behind him.

I noticed they hadn't even given us the command to beat him. But then it was probably that they realized no one would have dared. He looked as if he could have taken us all on at once. He was very tall and extremely muscular, with an ugly pockmarked face. He glared at us all for a moment and then immediately proceeded to demonstrate his own unique form of Kung fu, by banging his head as hard as he could against the pipes in the corner. Then suddenly he stopped and turned around, and let out a horrible sardonic laugh. I assume this was to let us know how strong he was and how much he could take.

He was also the worst of bullies. And mealtimes became somewhat of a nightmare, when he would demand that we all give him a share our meager portions of food. We were all starving already, especially the younger prisoners, but no one dared to protest.

One day, however, one of the younger cellmates had had enough!

"Forget it! I'm hungry myself!" he replied angrily and kept eating, after the bully had demanded his food. The next instant, the bully was on the other side of the cell, and on top of the younger man who was laid sprawled out on the floor with food all over him and a bloody nose. The guards heard the racket, and immediately our bully was hauled out of the cell. When he came back, he was in handcuffs. His behavior towards us wasn't any better, but at least now he couldn't hurt anyone.

However, I soon noticed that he could not easily eat, or wash himself, with the handcuffs on behind his back. He was forced to eat like a dog. And even though I didn't like him anymore than anyone else, God gave me compassion for him and I began to feed him at mealtimes. I also helped him wash his face, and go to the restroom. After about a month the guards took off his handcuffs. He still caused problems for the guards and showed nothing but contempt for the other prisoners. However, I had managed to gain his friendship and he left me alone. One day he even told me, "You're the only decent one in this whole stinking place!" I was grateful that God had used me to demonstrate His love and touch this man's heart.

Some of the younger criminals learned that I had been to the university and that I knew English. They asked me to teach them. It was risky, because if I were caught teaching English, the guards would have another reason to accuse me of being a counter-revolutionary. But I was so bored that I decided to take the risk. I would spell out English words for them to memorize, and even taught them a little grammar. Later we got a prisoner in our cell that had Mao's little red book in English. He let me borrow it, and I practiced my English by translating from English to Chinese and visaversa. This way I was able to keep my mind active and also improve my English

After about a year in prison I became severely ill. I had been given a shabby quilt upon entering prison and after so many months it had gotten quite filthy. I decided to take it apart and wash it. Unfortunately I knew nothing about quilts and when I sewed it back together I only sewed the outside. The batting soon balled up and rolled to the edges leaving me with only a thin covering during the cold winter. I would shiver all night long. The man who slept next to me had tuberculosis and as my resistance wore down, I became very ill. By the end of winter I was running a temperature of 103 degrees. The guards were afraid that I would infect my cellmates and so they sent me to the prison hospital.

Compared to the crowded filthy prison cells, the hospital seemed like heaven to me. I was given a bed all to myself with clean white sheets. We were even allowed to talk to one another. After a couple of weeks my fever went down, and I was able to move about the ward freely. I spent much of my time taking care of some of the terminally ill patients. Their families had abandoned many of them, and the hospital did not have nurses to attend to their needs. I would change their sheets when they lost control of their bladders or bowels. I would help them to sit up in bed, and picked them up off the floor if they fell. As a final act of mercy, I would put clean clothes on them after they had died. I tried to show them the love of Christ. It was the Cultural Revolution and I couldn't speak openly with them about Christ without being taken out immediately and shot. I hoped that they would understand, however, since I was in prison for being a Christian, what was motivating me and look to God. Many of these patients called my name during their final hours.

It was during this hospital stay that Dorothy first learned where I was. The prison officials contacted her and told her that I was ill and that she could bring me special foods. She wouldn't be allowed to see me, but just knowing that I was alive, and that she was able to help me, made all the difference. It was amazing that I had been in the same prison where she worked as a night parolee for all this time and she never even knew it. She worked on the other side of the prison, and had even been treated in this same hospital.

One Sunday I looked out the window and couldn't believe my eyes. Dorothy and our two boys were in the courtyard and had come to bring me food. Dorothy was hoping for a glimpse of me through a window. We saw each other at the same moment, and how our hearts were stirred. She pointed to the window and told my two boys, "There is your papa." The boys cried out together, "Papa!" But apparently I had lost so much weight, and had changed so drastically, that they were confused and turned to their mother and said, "That's not Papa."

For the first several weeks of my three-month stay in the hospital, Dorothy and I were able to see each other in this way. We couldn't speak to each other, but just looking on one another brought warmth and joy to our hearts. Soon, however, we were discovered by the guards, and in a fit of rage they boarded up all the windows. The next Sunday I heard Dorothy and the boys down in the courtyard. The boys were playing with a big, yellow dog and making lots of noise. It took some doing, but I finally found a crack in the plywood that I could see through. It broke my heart to see Dorothy and the boys turning away to leave so dejected looking. I couldn't be sure we would ever see each other again, since I was still waiting to be sentenced, possibly to death.

Our brief time of contact had been severed once again. At the end of three months the officials determined that I was well enough to return to my cell. With a heavy heart I rejoined my fellow inmates in the crowded dark hole.

God was using all these experiences to train me. The Bible says that we must deny ourselves, take up our cross, and follow Him. I had opportunities daily to apply this scripture. In the West when a person feels called to the ministry they usually decide to attend Bible School or Seminary. I had felt God's call to ministry, but in my case there were no Bible Schools, so God had fashioned one for me. Instead of studying homiletics, hermeneutics, Greek, and Hebrew, I was being taught the greater lessons of obedience, submission, forgiveness, love, endurance, and patience.

The Bible says that Jesus was numbered among the transgressors here on earth. In heaven He had had all glory, majesty, and power. And yet He was willing to come to earth as a man for our sake. Through self-sacrifice and submission he chose to live among sinful men for thirty-three and a half years.

Living day in and day out with criminals, I began to appreciate this more fully. I was there unwillingly. I wouldn't have stayed for a minute if I could have left. It nauseated me hearing their perverted stories and filthy language, continually. The more I thought about it, the more I was struck by the fact that Jesus loved sinners not only enough to be counted as one, but even to the point of taking their place by His death on a cross.

I knew that even if I could have, I wouldn't have died for my fellow inmates. I had only a little Christian compassion and not that kind of love. That would require "perfect love" and there is only one who has that type of love and His name is Jesus.

Chapter 15

Mr. Room Corner

I awoke with a sudden jolt to a nightmarish scene. It was pitch black and the whole room was shaking and vibrating around me. The noise was deafening and only eerie flashes of blinding light coming in from outside interrupted the total darkness. At first I thought the world was coming to an end until I realized what was happening. An extremely powerful earthquake had just struck.

It had been my turn to sleep on the end that night so I was the first one out of our communal bed. I jumped up, only to be immediately knocked to the floor. The others began piling out behind me, terrified, some screaming pitifully, even acknowledging God for the first time in their cries for help. I struggled to my feet, and looking towards the door, saw that it held fast. We were trapped inside with no escape!

As a geologist, I was knowledgeable about earthquakes. I had read that the most dangerous place in a room was the center. It was where the ceiling would fall in first. The corners were supported three dimensionally, and would hold up longer.

So I began shouting as loud as I could to everyone, "Get in the corners of the room! Everyone get in the corners!" With a great deal of effort I managed to get to a corner myself, and I continued calling to the others to do the same. But most of them must have thought I was crazy, and instead dove under the bouncing boards that made up our bed.

Then just as suddenly as it had started, the earthquake subsided, and the building settled back into place. The flashes from the natural electrical ground currents caused by the earthquake ceased. It was the middle of the night and we were in total darkness. The earthquake had knocked out all the power. The floor was soaking wet. Our urine bucket and washing water had been turned over. All over the prison we could hear the pitiful whining of wretched men pleading to be let out. The guards outside, sounding still quite shaken, groped along in the darkness and shouted back orders for everyone to keep quiet and stay where they were. Miraculously, the prison had survived very minimal damage.

I realized later that God had placed me in one of the most structurally sound buildings in the earthquake area. The thick concrete walls of the prison with its' T-shaped beams supporting the roof, held up, while most of the homes and buildings around us were destroyed.

For the rest of the time that I was in with these same cellmates, I was known as "Mr. Room Corner". I'm still not sure some were ever able to comprehend the structural dynamics involved no matter how simply I tried to explain it to them. All I could do was laugh with them and let them go on thinking that I had been frightened out of my mind, when I had tried to get them in the corner during the earthquake.

It was 3:42 in the morning on July 26, 1976, when the 8.1 magnitude earthquake had hit. This was the famous China earthquake that killed over a quarter of a million people. According to our history, the ancient Chinese emperors used to publicly humble themselves when natural disasters such as this occurred. They thought that they had done something wrong and had angered heaven. There is also an old Chinese superstition that when an emperor was about to die, a major natural disaster would occur.

Though Mao never publicly humbled himself, it was as if the earthquake had signaled his approaching death. There was only one news source in China at this time, and since the Communists controlled it, and it promoted the party line, we were allowed to read the newspapers in prison. I had been noticing for sometime that Mao was appearing less and less in photos. The few times his picture did appear he was sitting down, and looking feeble and half-paralyzed. It was in a way symbolic of what was happening in the country. As a nation we had become weak and paralyzed. The Cultural Revolution had now been going on for almost 10 years, and the country was nearly bankrupt. The young people that had been recruited by Mao, as part of his now failing revolution never finished their education. Today they are known as "The Lost Generation". So many of the nation's intellectuals had been imprisoned during this time that the country had lost ground in the sciences, education, and industrial technologies. Many hoped that once Mao died, there would be much needed reform.

But Mao was not the only problem. A group of four top leaders famously known as the "Gang of Four" had been the most responsible for zealously carrying out Mao's highly destructive policies. Mao's wife, Chiang Ching, led this group, which had also been responsible for the attacks on many of the high-ranking Communist officials threatening Mao. There is a saying in China that developed during that time, "Who will be sorry now? Who is number two?" They had helped Mao several times to get rid of his number two man, acting always in Mao's name, who was viewed as a god by the people.

The earthquake occurred just less than two months before Mao's death on September 9, 1976. The country set aside the entire following month to mourn his passing. At this time I had been in prison for over two years. I had been interrogated over fifty times, and yet no charges had ever been formally filed against me, or a trial held. In a democracy like America, this would be unheard of. The sixth amendment to the Constitution of the United States guarantees both a speedy and public trial. However, my situation was not uncommon for China. Many at this time had been held for years without a trial. It was a great irony that the Communists claimed to uphold Chinese law, which stated that all citizens have the right to a trial within three months.

Two weeks after Mao was dead, a guard came to my cell, and told me to "pack my luggage." Of course I didn't have any luggage, but this was the phrase they used to let us know that we were about to be sentenced. Prosecutors had at last made formal charges against me, and without any trial or defense, I was brought before the judge to receive my sentence. The judge, a court reporter, and myself were the only ones present.

The judge began coldly, "Number 390, though you still do not admit your guilt, we have proof that you have been involved in counter-revolutionary activities. You have conducted illegal church meetings in homes. You also oppose the Communist party, and have spoken against the leaders. And worst of all, you have blasphemed the great leader of our people, Chairman Mao. Therefore, I am sentencing you to fifteen years hard labor."

I was angry and began to tell him that the accusations were all false, but he quickly interrupted.

"Be quiet, or I'll sentence you to death, just like I did to the three Catholics last week." "None of your type deserve to live." And then pausing, he added cynically, "Of course, you can appeal if you like."

As I was being led away, I thought to myself, "you bet I'm going to appeal", even though I knew it would be futile. The same justice system that had just given me my sentence also dominated higher appeals and would rule the same way.

I was taken now to a new area of prison to await relocation to the labor camp. Here prisoners underwent several months of final indoctrination before leaving. I would have more opportunities, believe it or not, to study Mao's red book.

Once in the new cell I looked out of the bars and saw some prisoners who were being beaten severely by the guards. I asked my cellmates what they had done and they replied, "Oh, those are prisoners who have appealed." Over their horrible cries, I could faintly hear, from out in the streets beyond, the noise of mournful chanting for Chairman Mao. I laughed to myself, and thought, "All your power, Chairman Mao, has come to an end, and God is triumphant. Though my sentence is for 15 years, I believe what He has shown me, that I will not serve more than five years."

As I was still deep in thought, staring out the window, one of my new cellmates gently tapped me on the back and asked, "How many tons?"

Turning around, somewhat puzzled, I inquired back, "What do you mean? How many tons?"

"How many tons of steamed corn?" Another chimed in as though I would now know exactly what the other one was talking about.

I just stared at them wondering what kind of crowd I had been placed with now. Realizing that I didn't have a clue what they were talking about, they began to patiently explain. It was common knowledge that a person received the equivalent of one pound of steamed corn a day for food. After three years, a person would have eaten at least half a ton of steamed corn, while after six years, it would equal one ton. The prisoners here had begun to view a person's sentence in terms of the number of tons of steamed corn that they would eat.

After they finished explaining, I laughed, and calculated in my head what the judge had just sentenced me to. Then I said, "I guess I'll be eating about two and a half tons." But in my heart I believed that God would deliver me as He had promised. I then asked them, "How about you guys?"

They laughed and said, "we have no idea." Which obviously meant that they had been given life sentences.

Three weeks later while I was still waiting to be transported to the labor camp, I was surprised when I heard people shouting on the streets outside the prison, "Down with the Gang of Four". Later I read in the paper that the "Gang of Four" had been arrested and were to be tried. Three government leaders had carried out a coup against them. Everyone knew that the country had literally been brought to the brink of destruction through the policies of Chairman Mao. But no one dared to put the blame on the recently deceased demigod. The "Gang of Four" therefore, though only a little less deserving, became the scapegoat and received all the blame for the problems of the last ten years.

I thought then that it would only be a matter of time until I was released since one of my charges had been speaking against the leadership. Now the leadership was changing, and hopefully better times were in store for China. I couldn't help but think that if I had been sentenced a few weeks later, after the "Gang of Four" had been denounced, I might not have received this sentence. However, God was directing my steps, and what looked like merely poor timing, would later prove to be part of His perfect plan for me. He wanted me to complete "seminary" and to be made ready for the "works of service" He was preparing.

After nearly two and a half years in prison, I was tired, and had no idea what was awaiting me at the labor camp. I knew that many men died from the severe conditions. So I committed my life to God and braced myself for what was coming next.

Chapter 16

God's T-Joint

Our caravan slowly snaked its way along the dusty, bumpy road as we gradually made our way to the new prison labor camp. I had been awakened at five that morning and herded onto one of several buses that were waiting outside the prison. Once inside the bus we were forced to sit on the floor since all the seats had been removed. Without seats they could squeeze in more prisoners, and keep us away from the windows. We had only been told that we were going to be near a town, called Chianmotou about three hundred miles south of Tianjin. Averaging only thirty miles an hour, the trip took over twelve hours. Our three buses rocked along, sandwiched between the police in the front and soldiers armed with machine guns in the back.

Late that evening we arrived at the prison camp, which housed a large scrap iron and steel plant. Approaching the prison we could see the eerie orange glow of the steel smelting furnaces and smell the rank fumes of burning metal, which permeated the air. Surrounding the prison were high walls, covered in barbed wire, and look out towers manned with armed guards. Once inside the gates, we quickly filed out of the buses, and hastily lined up to receive instructions. Afterward, we marched to a set of grim looking buildings and were separated into small crowded cells.

From the beginning I was somewhat of an oddity among this crowd. Most of my fellow prisoners were desperate, hardened criminals, and they distrusted me because I was so different. My speech and manners, which appeared to them so "gentlemanly", were completely foreign to them. I did my best not to offend them and as time went by, it became less of an issue.

My days were now filled with difficult and exhausting work. However, it was an improvement to be doing something physical again, and the time passed much faster. In the prison in Tianjin we had been forced to sit quietly all day everyday studying Chairman Mao's teachings. The tedium of those two and a half years had almost driven me crazy. At least now, it was only in the evenings after our shift, that we were required to study Maoism.

The plant's function was to take in scrap iron, melt it down, mold it into various parts used for industrial piping, and then put it through a process of heating and cooling to strengthen it. The plumbing parts that we made the most were called T-joints. A T-joint connects three pipes together in the shape of a "T". I worked loading the newly molded T-joints onto carts that we then carried by overhead crane, and placed into annealing furnaces to be strengthened. Since these furnaces reached temperatures as high as 2700 degrees Fahrenheit, the heat from them was almost unbearable. Even with temperatures outside as cold as 10 degrees below freezing, inside, we worked stripped to the waist. Day after day, as I lifted heavy T-joints and placed them in the waiting trolleys, the iron dust, and the thick black smoke from the furnaces, was choking me, and making it nearly impossible to breathe. To my dismay I found that my asthma was returning.

As if the working conditions were not difficult enough, my co-workers were an even greater challenge. One day two of them had gotten into a terrible fight in my area. Suddenly, one of them picked up an iron bar and was about to smash the other one in the head with it. Though I was smaller than both and frightened half to death, I instinctively grabbed the man with the iron bar. "Do you want to be shot?" I hollered. "If you kill him, that's exactly what they'll do to you! Is anything worth that?"

Thankfully, he simmered down, and even told me later that he was grateful I had stopped him. It seemed I often intervened in their fights and even gained the respect of some. But at times they would suddenly turn on me and with scowling faces begin deriding and bullying me. Those times were very difficult, and I used to want to turn and run, but somehow God gave me the courage to face them.

One day Captain Liu, who was in charge of the prison, called me into his office to ask me if I would teach him English. He had read in my files that I was a college graduate like himself. I gathered he needed the intellectual stimulation. So periodically I would go to his office, though I don't think he cared that much about learning English, because many times we just talked or played Chinese chess. I was usually exhausted after an eight-hour shift in the iron plant, but tried my best to stay alert. From our times together I soon learned that he was very lonely and hated the work he was doing. Some of the other prisoners, seeing the favor I was getting, began flattering me in front of Captain Liu, hoping that I would put in a good word for them.

We were served more food here than at the prison in Tianjin, but unfortunately, the nutritive quality of the food was even less. We were hardly ever given meat and had become quite depleted of protein. The prisoners, however, had developed an ingenious way to supplement their diet. I discovered this one warm evening.

I was in my cell that night after having completed my shift, dutifully studying Mao's little red book, when one of the guards came to my door and ordered me outside. The guards had been keeping chickens, and would get the prisoners to gather bugs to feed them with. They handed me a big cloth bag and sent me about the grounds to fill it with bugs.

As I came around the corner of a building which contained several furnaces, I noticed some prisoners standing behind one, and hidden from the guards' sight. They motioned for me to come over.

"Hey 390, try one of these," one of them whispered and handed me something hot and crispy.

"What is it?" I asked.

"Don't worry about it, just eat it!" he insisted.

Obediently, I took a small bite. It tasted a bit like dried shrimp, but even better. I quickly scooped a whole handful off the top of the furnace and devoured them.

"What was it?" I asked again, crunching a mouthful.

They smiled somewhat mischievously and then one of them pointed to my bag of bugs. I swallowed hard at the thought of it but immediately decided to ignore it, and continued eating heartily. We were so protein deprived that we craved anything even resembling meat. The chickens would just have to share.

The food we were served was made from hybrid sorghum. It was the only thing that grew well in that part of China. We ate it in steamed bread form, and in a type of porridge. Though it was very bland and lacking in nutrition, at least we were served large portions, since the guards wanted us to have strength to work.

After I had been at the labor camp for a year, Dorothy was notified that she would be allowed to come see me. It was now over three years since we had spoken. In all this time the only contact I had had was to wave at her and the boys from my hospital room in the prison in Tianjin. Though it was almost impossible to make such a trip in her circumstances she did it out of her great love for me.

The next Saturday night after working all week at her prison labor job, Dorothy went home, put on her best dress, and gathered up all the delicious foods that she had prepared for me. It took her eight hours by train to get to Chianmotou, the town closest to the prison. She had arrived before dawn, and then had to walk for two hours to reach the prison. Since she arrived before the official visiting hours she had to wait even longer outside the prison walls.

At about a quarter to nine that morning, the guards came and took some of us to the visiting room so that we would already be there when the visitors were let in. About nine the door opened, and the most precious person in the world to me, walked in. She looked so calm and peaceful as she made her way across the room and took her seat across the table from me. That was as close as we could get and touching one another was strictly prohibited. In this way the guards made sure that the visitors did not secretly transfer any items to the prisoners.

My arms ached to hold her, and I struggled to keep a tight reign on my emotions. I had to be on guard that I wouldn't reveal anything that could harm Dorothy or her father. The guards stood behind us, monitoring every word. I put my finger to my lips indicating that I had admitted nothing during the interrogations. Dorothy understood this since she was a prisoner herself and nodded her head knowingly. We just sat for a moment looking at each other across the 3-foot wide table; there was so much to say that we didn't know where to begin.

"So how is your father?" I ventured to ask, trying to sound as nonchalant as possible for the sake of the guards.

"He's fine," she replied, just as coolly.

"And the boys," I asked. "How are they doing?"

"They're doing well. In fact I've been receiving a little help financially for them from your father. He's been sending us a little money each month now that his situation has improved."

I was glad to hear this. Though my parents had been faithful to the Communists since they took over in 1949, like most other intellectuals, they also had become victims of the Cultural Revolution. Their previous associations with the West had made them especially suspect and the Red Guards had persecuted them. They had been severely "criticized" in the Communist fashion and lost their respected positions in society. This had been so traumatic for my mother that in 1971, she had a heart attack and died in her sleep. She had never really grasped the true evil nature of Communism, and my father had only recently accepted that the Communist ideals were at fault. Now that Mao was dead and the Cultural Revolution was officially over, my father had been restored by the Communists. One sign that he had relented towards me somewhat was that he was now sending my boys support, knowing that I couldn't take care of them.

All too quickly our short 20-minute allotted visit was over. The guards searched the food thoroughly that Dorothy had brought, their hands tearing apart candies wrapped in paper. They even stirred through the toothpaste she had brought me. But nothing could take away from the love that she had expressed to me by preparing those things.

I sat and watched as they led Dorothy out of the room. In some ways the visit had been so unsatisfactory. It was the first time we had spoken in three years. Under the pressure of the meeting we had hardly been able to say anything. And now I wouldn't see her again for six months. I knew that in the days to come I would replay our visit over and over in my mind. I never could get over the fact that Dorothy had suffered so much physically for her faith, and yet still looked so beautiful.

It wasn't long after this visit that I became quite discouraged. My health was deteriorating quickly. I had developed pleurisy, and breathing became increasingly more difficult and painful. I actually began to complain to God. "Lord, you promised me that I would not be in this place more than five years. But I've been sentenced to fifteen years. If I have to labor here that long, I will die." I pleaded with Him daily to deliver me and longed for another word from Him to hang onto."

But God didn't answer me for many days. Many Christians have gone through times where it seems as if their prayers hit the ceiling. They feel a desperate need to hear from the Lord, and yet hear nothing. I grew frustrated, and felt forgotten. Everything in life seemed to be going wrong. I had lost everything for his sake. Why was this happening to me?

It wasn't until much later that I finally realized the trap I had fallen into by feeling sorry for myself. Then I understood. God was trying to bless me. He was helping me to grow from being a baby or carnal Christian into a spiritually mature one. I had to learn to submit fully to His will no matter what it entailed. I had been submitting up to a point for years, but now God seemed to be requiring me to yield to Him all the way. Would I still love and trust

Him, even when I couldn't sense His presence? What if I did die here in this prison? If that was His plan for me, was I willing?

Then one day it happened again, that God spoke to my heart. Working among the furnaces, I had noticed that sometimes, when the fire wasn't regulated properly and was too hot, the T-Joint simply melted in the furnace. That day, while loading the furnaces, God drew my attention to the melting T-joint. He assured me that He would "control the duration and the temperature of the fire," and that I would "not be destroyed or melted down like the T-joints." But He would "deliver me". He wanted me to completely yield my will to His. I thought of Job and knew that I too needed to repent in my own dust and ashes, those of the dirty scrap iron plant. When I did I was totally "delivered". In the fiery furnace, I was God's T-joint.

Not long after I had completed my second year at the labor camp, Captain Liu called me into his office to tell me that I would be allowed to appeal my case. I had been classified as a political prisoner, though in truth my case was never "political". However, the particular class of political prisoners that I fell into was now being released and restored. This was happening now that the former Communist leader,

Deng Xiao-Ping had also been released and restored and was assuming more power. I was told to write my appeal secretly since only our class of prisoners was being considered. Most of the prisoners at our iron plant would not qualify and Captain Liu didn't want a riot on his hands. I used the ten minute breaks that I had while the T-joints were in the furnace to write my appeal. The hope of freedom is very motivating and within a just a few days I had written over ten thousand words.

For several months I heard nothing. Then on the morning of November 8, 1978 one of the police captains approached me and told me that I would be released that day. Within two hours I was headed for the train station with a policeman from Tianjin and on my way home. Once a prisoner was released they were ushered out of the prison as quickly as possible so they wouldn't cause trouble among the other inmates.

I had been in prison for a total of four and a half years. God had spoken to my heart that first evening that I wouldn't be imprisoned for more than five years. Praise the Lord! Like Shadrach, Meshach, and Abednego, I too, in a unique way, had experienced the protective power of the Son of Man in the fiery furnace, and came out unharmed. Not even the smell of smoke remained.

Chapter 17

Restored

The car picked up speed again as we entered onto the main road and raced the short distance left from the police station in Tianjin to Dorothy's home. The trip couldn't have gone by fast enough, as far as I was concerned. Ten hours after leaving the prison camp, and after an all night train ride, we pulled up in front of the home where my family was now living. My sons saw me through the window and amazingly enough, recognized me after four and a half years. They had been only a little over two years old when I was arrested and now they were almost seven. Those were lost years, but God was getting ready to make them up to me.

I was able to stay with my family in Tianjin, until the date of my court hearing. At the hearing I was officially exonerated of all accusations against me. My verdict was over-turned, and all charges were dismissed. The next day an elderly judge and his younger col-league escorted me back to Beijing. It was rather an emotional moment for me as I walked through the large doors of the Institute of Geology, and reported to my old workplace. The judges had come there to conduct a mass meet-ing. Once again I was paraded to the front of the same large hall, and stood before all my for-mer colleagues. But this time things were dif-ferent. The elder, more distinguished looking judge stepped up to the podium and the room became respectfully silent. As he began to speak I felt the heaviness of years of pain and suffering, being lifted from me. It was as though the Lord was present in that room and I could hear him saying to me, "well done good and faithful servant". The old judge concluded his brief statement, stepped down from the podium, and walked slowly to his seat as the crowd quietly looked on. That was all there was to it. Freddie Sun was fully restored as a respected member of the Institute of Geology.

Not long afterwards, I was told that as part of my reinstatement, the Institute would pay me back the entire amount I would have received if I had been working for the last four and a half years. I received the equivalent of almost fifteen hundred US dollars. This was a considerable amount of money when exchanged into the Chinese currency. The first thing I did was go out and buy presents for the whole family.

All over the country intellectuals were now in great demand. The great "brain drain" that resulted from the Cultural Revolution had created a shortage of educated and trained people in the workplace. I even found out later on, that one of the vice-presidents of the Chinese Academy of Sciences, had been telling the Public Security Bureau in Tianjin that if they did not release Freddie Sun, "he would send people from Beijing to go pick him up." Mao's "experiment" had failed. Furthermore, it had produced a whole generation of young people that were uneducated. It was time for change.

As I returned to work, I found that most of my coworkers were very gracious towards me. God had given me the grace to forgive them, and I was able to quickly put the past behind me. However, apparently God intended for me to be a witness of His justice as well as His mercy. He says in His Word, "Vengeance is mine, I will repay", and this seemed particularly applicable in the case of two of my coworkers who had denounced me the strongest, and with unusual cruelty. Both had gone through what appeared to be a divine judgement. The first was a woman who had worked with me for some time in the lab. She had been extremely zealous, and accused me furiously at my public denouncement in 1968. Later, when I was in prison, she spitefully threw out all of my possessions that were still at the institute. However, not long afterwards, her husband suddenly died. Others told me that the shock of it and the grief she had suffered caused her hair to turn prematurely white. Unfortunately, she was still full of hatred towards me, and feared that I would try to take revenge. Little did she understand that the very God she rejected gave me the grace to forgive her.

The other coworker was a man who now worked in the same lab as myself. He had also been very cruel in his denouncements of me, and suffered similar hardships. His wife had died suddenly from an illness, and when he married a second woman she was hit by a car and also died. He himself then became very ill and had to have one of his kidneys removed. Later he developed heart disease, and was now so debilitated he no longer was able to do field work.

Soon after I was restored, the Communists elected Deng Xiao-Ping as the new leader of

China. He had had an on again, off again relationship with Mao since the beginning of Mao's rule. He had been one of the top leaders of the Communist party and was well respected by many for his more balanced approach to government. He was still a Communist however, and like Mao believed that force was necessary to change the country. He had been a successful military leader, and had proven himself many times over in the most difficult assignments. The Communists knew that they needed a leader like Deng to get the country back on track. The change in government led to the release of over 600,000 intellectuals like myself who had been wrongly accused since 1957.

Also at this time, an incident occurred that greatly impacted my life and propelled me a great deal forward in my career. Science had become very popular with the Communists as they began to realize their need to progress. Deng was now promoting science as a "productive force". The government decided to hold the largest scientific symposium in the history of the country. Focusing on the Tibetan Plateau, this symposium would be international in scope and include all different branches of science. After the symposium was completed, the Academy would arrange an international expedition to the Tibetan Plateau.

I had been brought into the preparations for the symposium almost from the first day I returned to the Institute because of my knowledge of English and background in geology. At that time there were very few people in China who spoke fluent English. And although my English was quite rusty after years of disuse, in comparison to most others, I sounded almost fluent. We prepared for this big event for a whole year. I sent out the letters of invitation and familiarized myself with the backgrounds of the international guests. I also set up their accommodations and even picked them up from the airport. Two days before the big event, The Chinese Academy of Sciences announced that the new leader and "Number One Man" in China, Deng, had decided to hold a reception for the international visitors. Deng, of course, spoke no English, and this caused everyone to scurry like mad to arrange an interpreter for the reception. The next day I was summoned into one of the director's offices.

"Mr. Sun," he began quite congenially, and putting me a little more at ease. "I've been told that you lived in America for a year and are rather fluent in English." He paused for a moment and smiled. I could only assume from his tone that it was now considered a good thing to have lived in America, and marveled a bit to myself how quickly God could turn things around. Then he asked. "Would you be interested in acting as the interpreter for Mr. Deng tomorrow at the reception?"

I couldn't believe the opportunity that had just been presented to me. Just a little over a year ago I had been a slave laborer in prison, loading heavy pieces of iron into burning hot furnaces all day, and now I was going to be interpreting for the number one man in China. I knew though that it was going to take some serious praying on my part to be able to do this. But I tried my hardest to reply as nonchalantly as possible, "Ah, sure, why not."

The next day I stood next to Mr. Deng Xiao-Ping while the guests filed past him at the reception. I translated the greetings of each guest and told Mr. Deng which branch of science they represented. In spite of the fact that it had been so long since I had used my English, God helped me to understand and translate accurately. Unknown to me, TV cameras were rolling and Deng and I would be featured on the national news that evening. China had been closed off from the rest of the world for so long that these first ventures in normal international relations were greeted with great fanfare.

The result for me after appearing on the national news with Deng was that my status at the Institute suddenly rose dramatically. When I walked into the lab the next morning I was greeted with a lot of good-natured teasing.

"Hey, here comes Freddie Sun the VIP" one called out.

Another said, "Freddie how about getting a favor for me from Deng."

From this point on my relationship with my colleagues was greatly improved. Any lingering suspicions about my past or questions in their minds about why I had been in prison now seemed to be completely gone. I found that even the Communists in the Security Department, trusted me now. They thought that I was one of them now and must be politically trustworthy to have "hung out" with Deng. Just as Psalm 23 says, 'You will prepare a table for me in the presence of my enemies.' I had walked through the valley of the shadow of death and was now enjoying the unmerited favor of God. Praise His holy Name!

After the symposium, the Academy asked me to participate in the Tibetan Plateau International Expedition. As a geologist, it was the opportunity of a lifetime. Right away I was put in charge of translation, interpretation, foreign affairs, scientific matters, and logistics. Later on I even handled the finances and personnel. The first expedition was so successful that it led to many others. And in the years between 1980 through 1988, I helped lead seven different expeditions to Tibet. Five of those years were in cooperation with the Royal Society of London and included distinguished Geo-scientists from the U.S. and Switzerland.

God blessed my career so much that I was soon traveling to foreign countries to attend as well as interpret for scientific symposiums. At first it was very challenging for me because I lacked the vocabulary for what was being taught by the instructors. But as time went by my ability to speak English improved greatly. Also, I had lost ten years of my career, and had forgotten much of what I had learned as a geology student. But now I was relearning from some of the top men in my field. By the end of 1988, ten years after I had been restored to my former position at the institute, by the grace of God, my knowledge of geology had exceeded that of my former colleagues. I became an expert in the fields of paleontology, evolutionism, stratiography, and catastrophism. I can speak as an authority to Chinese intellectuals brainwashed by atheism on the topic of why there is no contradiction between the Bible and science. I can also explain why Darwin's Theory of Evolution is an out of date hypothesis. All this is the result of God moving so powerfully in my life to restore me in my career. It was not simply due to my own personal efforts; rather, it was God who had restored and even promoted me. He had begun by orchestrating it for me to stand beside Deng for several hours. Deng never again appeared at a convention like this and had only done it then to let the public know that he was back in power. But because of that one event, many doors had been opened to me. How much better will it be however, when one day we stand beside Jesus in heaven and God restores to us everything that we lost for His sake, plus so much more, for all of eternity.

The ten years following my release from prison saw many other blessings as well. My aunt who had denied the Lord during the Cultural Revolution repented of her unbelief. It was so precious to me to see her join in the fellowship again. Her husband, (my Uncle Gordon) who had been willing for us to meet those many years ago in his home, even when he wasn't a Believer, also gave his life to the Lord. Soon after my release I was able to take Dorothy and the boys to meet my father. He had been restored to his former position but was now in poor health. He was very happy to see us, and even talked somewhat freely about things that the Communists had done wrong. He did not accept the Lord while we were there, but seeds were planted and I can only hope that he turned to the Lord before he died in 1980. I leave him in the Lord's hands.

Even on top of all these blessings, there was more that God was going to do in my life. He was about to lead me into the ministry that He had called me to many years before.

Chapter 18

China Ministry

In 1980, after having been imprisoned for twenty years of her life, Dorothy was finally released and her record cleared. She had entered prison as a young woman in her twenties and was now in her forties. Since she had been a student before her arrest the government determined that she had lost no wages. Officially it was now recognized that she had been wrongfully accused, but she was not recompensed one cent for twenty years of hard labor.

However, God was about to bless Dorothy through unusual circumstances in much the same way He had blessed me. She had heard about a job in Beijing with the World Health Organization. The position was for someone who could speak English and was knowledge-able of medicine. Since she was still in college at the time of her arrest, she had never completed her medical degree. Also she had not spoken English for almost twenty years. It seemed impossible for her to get the job, but just the same, she prepared as best she could for the interview. When she met the other applicants on the day of the interview she realized immediately that they were all more qualified than she was.

The interviewing committee consisted of several Communist officials and one Westerner. The Westerner noticed the twenty-year gap in Dorothy's resume, and asked her about it. Dorothy wasn't sure how to answer him. After years of imprisonment and oppression by the Communists, she was afraid to say anything that they might hold against her. She looked over at the Communist officials in the room and asked them if she could tell where she had been. They nodded their approval. Dorothy then briefly told her story of how she had been imprisoned for the last twenty years, and why. Several days later she received notice of the results of the interview. Miraculously, she had been chosen for the position over all the other, more qualified applicants. She realized that God had used her story to touch that man's heart and he had persuaded the others to hire her. God had worked supernaturally in her behalf. Dorothy and the boys were now able to join me in Beijing and we all moved into an apartment together. This was the first time in our married lives that we lived together for more than three months. It was a time of much happiness for us.

The next four years passed by peacefully and without much incident until one day when Dorothy returned home from work with some startling news.

"Freddie, boys, listen!" She said excitedly, "The most amazing thing has happened. I've been offered a position to be a visiting scholar at the University of North Carolina in the United States. I don't understand why they would want me, but they do. I don't even have a college education, and though my English has improved, it still isn't that good!" Then pausing for a moment to catch her breath, she added, "Of course, I can't even think of breaking up our family again. But God has given me this favor, and I don't know what to do."

For a few minutes we just sat staring at her. Then suddenly we all began to speak at once. Somehow over the noise, I was able to make myself heard, "Wait a minute everybody, we have to pray about this. This could be a door that God is opening up for us. It's true we would have to be separated again for a while, but this could be a way for us to move to the United States just as we have hoped and planned for several years now. Just think what it would mean. You boys wouldn't have to grow up under the same horrible conditions and lack of freedom that we have had to endure."

We began soon after that an intense time of prayer, and seeking of God's direction. A few days later we felt that the Lord had showed us that Dorothy was to take the position. We had no idea of what God was planning for the future but we sensed that He was moving and we must follow Him.

It was 1984, and once again we faced separation, as Dorothy moved to North Carolina to begin her new job. She gave lectures at the University of North Carolina on "Public Health in China", and began working on obtaining permanent residence status in the United States.

Back in China, I took care of the boys, and also continued to travel extensively with my geological work at the institute. During this time I found myself thinking a lot about how the Lord had called me into the ministry years ago. Almost thirty years had gone by, and I had spent a lot of time learning from the Lord, but I still had done very little ministry. However, that was about to change.

In 1987 I traveled to Hawaii to represent China at an energy resources conference. The iron curtain surrounding China was beginning to open slightly by this time and I was allowed to travel on business more freely. After the conference I was able to travel to North Carolina to visit Dorothy. We had a wonderful reunion. Since coming to the U.S. she had dedicated her life to working full-time for the Lord. I felt that the Lord was also telling me, that now too was the time for me to enter into full-time ministry. The boys and I would have to wait another year for Dorothy to receive official residency status, but then we would all be together again for our new life in America.

At this same time we were introduced to Bob Finley. He had served one year as a missionary to China until in 1949 all the missionaries had to leave. He had founded an indigenous missions support organization called Christian Aid Mission, which supports individuals and organizations reaching their own people in countries all over the world. He had a great love for the Chinese people and a strong desire to help them. He said to me, "Freddie, since you are going back to China, see if you can find some young Watchman Nee's or Wang Mintao's for us to help. Try to find the true Churches in China. We have been praying for

China for many years. We would like to support the gospel work there."

It was at this point that the Lord started me in full-time ministry. I had been in contact with various members of house churches for thirty years. After China began to open up in the early eighties the intense persecution of the prior years relaxed somewhat and the house church movement began spreading like wildfire. After I returned to Beijing, God began moving powerfully, leading me to make contacts with House Church leaders from regions all over China. At that time I also assisted in Bible smuggling operations and helped bring into China over one hundred thousand Bibles per year.

In 1988, Dorothy received her official residency status in the United States and the boys and I were able to join her. At last we were reunited as a family, and this time it seemed for good. As I was flying from China to the U.S. I realized that God was using me like a T-joint, linking me on one end with China and on the other with America and the West.

We began immediately our present "T-joint" ministry of working to support the spread of the Gospel in China. In 1992, we were able to travel back to China for the first time and we quickly learned that one of the greatest needs of the Church in China is to train workers. God led us to support indigenous Bible Schools in China. He has enabled us to help establish 66 Bible Schools, training over 20,000 Christian leaders each year, as of the time of this writing. We soon hope to have a Bible School in every province of China.

The Communists have been trying to eradicate Christianity in China for over a half century. When they took over the country in 1949, there were approximately one million Christians. After having been ruthlessly persecuted for over fifty years many estimate that the church in China has now close to one hundred million Christians. This tremendous growth has been what has spurred the need for more trained workers.

Christian leaders are trained in both underground and officially recognized Bible schools in China. Underground training schools make up two thirds of the works that we support. These schools meet in secret. Most of them are rural, and have some sort of front to them. For example, in one province a school we help support meets in a pig farm. The owner of the farm is known to get very upset if visitors come around and disturb his pigs. Of course the real reason is that in the back of his property there are students being trained in the Bible.

Another Bible school we help support first met in the leader's home, Brother Jin. There were forty students studying in his school, when Jin was arrested and put in prison for three years. His students spread out into nearby towns and God added to their numbers as other leaders continued the training. Eventually there were nine different schools operating with approximately ten students in each school. Not only was Jin able to lead 26 prisoners to the Lord while he was in prison, but his school more than doubled. And since 1992, this school has trained over 800 Christian Workers.

The remaining, approximately one third of the Bible schools we help support, are officially recognized and part of the government's Three-Self Patriotic Movement. In these cases however the leaders have taken a bold stance against government intervention. Many of them are younger pastors who hold to the fundamental teachings of the Bible, and have so far remained free from government control in their particular province. Every province in China is different, and in a few there are so many Christians, and they are so well respected, that there is much freedom.

One example of how God is working powerfully in the different provinces occurred recently. The local government ordered the army to dynamite or bulldoze all the unregistered church buildings in a particular area. However, as proof of God's judgement, all eight of the men who participated in the destruction of one of the churches in this area died afterwards. Four of them died almost immediately, and the remaining four, seeing this, fled with fright only to die later, one after another. The believers in the area were so emboldened by this, that some wrote in huge letters outside of the apartment buildings they live in, the word "Emanuel" (God is with us!).

Some of the leaders with whom we partner are actually ex-Communists. In Inner Mongolia we work with a highly respected man known as Elder Gao. The testimony of his conversion is very interesting. His wife had become very ill but was healed after much prayer by some local Christians. He had been an atheist all of his life and had no need in his mind for Jesus. However, he allowed his wife to attend church, and although he walked there with her, he would wait outside until the meeting was over. Once or twice however, he went inside the church and was so touched on these occasions by the Spirit of God, that he was moved to tears. But he continued to harden his heart, and one day when his wife asked him to pray with her, he shouted at her angrily, "I don't want to pray!" That night however, while he was sleeping a great light came through his window and knocked him to the floor, and a voice calling his name spoke to him and said, "You pray!" He was terrified and knew instantly that God was real, and was to be feared and obeyed. Since that time he has become a strong Christian leader and has planted more than twenty churches with congregations ranging between five hundred to a thousand people. He runs schools that are currently training over five hundred gospel workers.

By God's grace we're assisting ministries all across China. In far-western China we support a work started by a man named Brother Zhao. Over fifty years ago he walked over two thousand miles to minister to Muslim Turks who live on the far-western border in China. He now trains workers and sends them to the churches that he has planted in that remote area.

These are just a few examples of the high caliber of Christian leaders and Bible schools that we have the privilege of supporting. Providing Bible teaching and discipling materials for our brothers and sisters in China is our greatest concern. Also there are an estimated five hundred million children in China. And since the government restricts families to only one child, these children tend to become the princes and princesses of their homes. The children receive whatever they ask. Even if they suddenly decide they want to go to Sunday school or have a Bible story read to them, unbelieving parents willingly agree. In response to this unique situation, we are training hundreds of teachers for Children's Sunday schools all over China. We are seeing tremendous fruit from this ministry as God uses these children to bring whole families to Christ.

Every year now I travel throughout China to establish new contacts with Christian leaders and verify the effectiveness of existing works supported by our ministry. We also purchase as many Bibles and Christian books as possible, and smuggle them into China. The workers are plentiful, but those helping to send them are few. Literally thousands of Chinese Christian workers are currently waiting to be trained and sent out to reach over one billion of their fellow countrymen. Over half a century ago, Western missionaries sowed the seeds of the Gospel, and the church in China watered them with her own blood. Today God is blessing with a great and plentiful harvest.

God is faithful and answers prayer. During the fiery trials He took everything from us, but time. Today however, he has restored it all and with a double blessing. He has even made up for the lost years in prison by seemingly slowing down our aging. Dorothy and I look younger than our years and enjoy good health and strength. Each year we travel thousands of miles together, spending eight or nine months away from home. We have everything we could ask for, especially the love of so many brothers and sisters in Christ. The only thing we need more of now is time.

An Opportunity to Get Involved

If you have been stirred by the reading of this book and would like to know more about how you can help to train, equip, and support native Chinese Christian church planters to reach their fellow countrymen with the Gospel, we would love to hear from you. Today the most effective way to impact the nation of China for Christ is to provide prayer and support for the thousands of Chinese Christians called by God to minister to the lost and unreached peoples of their homeland. American churches and individual Christians must consider more than simply supporting the sacrificial efforts of the relatively few westerners in China sent out as teachers of English or as "tent-makers". We must partner with the established church in China if the country is ever to be reached.

God has raised up this ministry as an efficient, safe and effective vehicle for individuals and churches in America to directly assist with the financial needs of churches and Bible schools in China. Those who send $30 per month or more for worker support will receive the name and photograph of a Chinese Christian church planter to pray for. Gifts may also be designated for building Bible schools or providing teaching materials. Please contact us at:

Christian Aid Mission
P.O. Box 9037
Charlottesville, VA 22906
Phone: 1-800-977-5650

E-mail: ask@christianaid.org

Website: www.christianaid.org

Member: Evangelical Council for Financial
Accountability (ECFA)

Appendix
_____

Poems by Freddie Sun

Authors Note: Some of these poems were composed while in prison, others after my release. The poems are written using both the "Gu Shi" (an ancient Chinese style) and a special pattern known as "Chi".

My First Night in Jail, May 5, 1974

Cold, cruel, handcuffs
biting into my hands.
The police car whistling along,
traveling to a black and gray castle.
A gray castle,
with iron gates
and heavy locks.
Before me I witness
torturing, kicking, and screaming.
The path leading to heaven is narrow
and those who find it are few.
A sleepless night flopping back and forth
but the dawn never comes.
The dawn never comes.
I hear only the steps of the guards
and my heart burns with desperation and sorrow.

The Plum Flower Tree

Note: In February 1976, I was threatened to be sentenced to death, so I compared and regarded myself as a plum tree, which is the national flower.

A night of snow and rain,
the winds howl,
and yet, standing erect in the yard is the plum tree,
isolated.
The bitter cold is
made worse by gusting winds.
But even the swirling ice and snow
can't stop the plum tree from blooming.
All other flower buds tightly shut out the cold,
while the plum tree flower petals open and
then
drop on the ground willingly to be buried in the
mud.
They dare to declare that an early spring is
approaching.
When all the flowers will bloom, they compete,
in brilliant color and fragrantly sweet.
But now one tries to find the plum flower and the
tree.
It is already gone,
It is even hard to find its shadow, in death.

Praising the Saints

From the ancient past
to the recent,
we review the history of the saints.
They are like the shining, twinkling stars in the sky.
Like rainbows
so colorful,
so bright.
Abraham, maintained his first faith and belief.
Joseph, endured for long
Moses, led Israelites across the Red Sea
David, ruled God's kingdom
Prophets, foretold
and three young men
were thrown into the fiery furnace.
Daniel, an administrator
was sent into the lions' den
and proved his innocence before God and man.
And they were all conquerors or victors
Because
God is with us today, yesterday, and tomorrow.
God's Word is the truth
for all eternity.
Jesus Christ came into the world
died on the cross,
and rose again.
His wondrous grace
attracts sinners so much,

that
they abandon the world and dedicate themselves
to the great commission.
Peter, was the pillar of the church
Paul, was the messenger
John, shared the Revelation.
They all saw the Son of Man wearing a white robe.
They put down God's Word in scripture.
The gospel spread
witnessed by the blood of martyrs'.
Martin Luther brought reform in the Middle Ages
And evil will eventually be
done away with.
The path leading to paradise is narrow.
We should run quickly and be blessed by the
Lord's love.
Who would win the gold medal in this race?

Visiting Europe in 1984

Note: At that time Dorothy, my wife, had already come
to the United States. In geological history, Europe and
North America were the same ancient continent, Then
the Atlantic Ocean opened up and separated the two.

Blue waves and green surges of
the great Atlantic Ocean
push against each other.
The tide of my heart is also high

as I stand at the shore of the British Isle.
Just as in the geological past
the continents of Europe and
North America
were one,
my wife and I were meant to be
as one.
But now, at present, only white sea gulls carry my prayer and praise
to the other shore.
On the opposite shore of the Atlantic,
in a university,
hidden on a green lawn
is my devout lady.
Though we have experienced water and fire
now we have learned much and become wise.
Our vision broadens.
We can even look back calmly to the sufferings
that we endured.
On to Switzerland I travel.
The snowy peaks
declare their praise to God.
I step on the sources of four rivers on the peak.
Water runs thousands of miles into the sea,
towards the north, south, east and west.
My soul goes along carrying His message.
In due time, He will bless us
Why should we sigh,
that the oceans and many barriers separate us.

God will cause us to cross the ocean
to make friends in all nations
and to bring news of peace and prosperity.

The Macedonian Call

Note: I once again receive the vision and calling.

Where can we find the beautiful steps of the
Apostles?
It is between Asia and Europe where the Aegean
Sea connects the two continents.
I look down from the plane
hundreds of miles below me
where many green islands
flash like pearls on the sea
and my mind goes back,
back to ancient times.
Many were their tribulations, sufferings, and labors.
The Apostles risked their lives every day.
In the wilderness,
they traveled,
by rivers and sea,
often at night.
But how
could they deny
the vision
shown

from heaven?
Though they were in bondage,
and prisoners,
they still carried out
the Lord's great commission.
The Macedonians crying
"Please help and rescue us"
stabbed their hearts.
So led by the Lord,
the Apostles boldly moved forward.
Now the ancient church buildings,
are only
rubble,
crumbling pillars,
and broken walls.
The goat skins record the life changing messages
of Apostles
It was a broken boat,
and floating wooden boards
that rescued one of the Apostles.
However, he landed on the shore of Europe.
And since then the gospel has been spreading
to four corners of the world
Now the same call
echoes
across the Pacific.
Who will hear the cry and accept the call
to lost souls in Asia.

Revisiting the United States (after thirty-seven years) in the autumn of 1987

I left North America long ago;
now I return,
and step on the land of this great continent.
The old friendly feeling remains
As I make many new acquaintances.
We give the testimony of a fiery trial and
the burden in our hearts lightens.
Each one shares his vision and we find common
ground.
A couple who experienced many tribulations
are joyfully reunited again.
And my bride dressed so pretty
To welcome the groom.
We experience another honeymoon.
Our small family has been dedicated
to the Lord.
The dark crosses we received were actually
invitations by God to be blessed.
We constantly prayed
to be able to understand
the grace from God hidden behind the crosses.
Today,
we are still in the dream,
together,
chatting forever.
But we have to part again

to do God's work across the sea.
In ancient times the church was blooming in Asia
Minor.
And today, where will God's house prosper?
China's call echoes across the Pacific
and spreads to other continents
Soul harvest in China is indeed ripe
Who will
labor
for the Lord
and store the harvest
in the barn?

MAN IN THE FIERY FURNACE

MAN IN THE FIERY FURNACE